# COMING CLEAN
## LIVING WITH OCD

**HAYLEY LEITCH**
WITH VERONICA CLARK

JOHN BLAKE

Published by John Blake Publishing Ltd,
3 Bramber Court, 2 Bramber Road,
London W14 9PB, England

www.johnblakepublishing.co.uk

www.facebook.com/Johnblakepub [f]
twitter.com/johnblakepub [t]

This edition published in 2014

ISBN: 978 1 78219 917 5

British Library Cataloguing-in-Publication Data:

A catalogue record for this book is available from the British Library.

Design by www.envydesign.co.uk

Printed and bound in Great Britain by CPI Group (UK) Ltd

3 5 7 9 10 8 6 4 2

ART

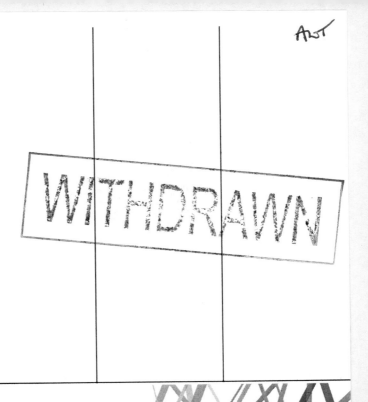

Get **more** out of libraries

**Please return or renew this item by the last date shown.**

**You can renew online at www.hants.gov.uk/library**

**Or by phoning  0845 603 5631**

Hampshire
County Council

For Nanny Linda and Nanny Rose – the finest
women I have ever known.

# *CONTENTS*

COMING
CLEAN
LIVING WITH OCD

## CHAPTER 1

# NANNY ROSE

STRETCHING OUT MY feet and legs, I used all my might to push my body upwards. Arching my back and dipping my head down, I did it again and again until I'd gained a little momentum. The chain of the swing was old and rusty so it took a little effort but, after four or five attempts, I suddenly began to rock back and forth until finally I was airborne. My skirt billowed out like a small white balloon and my lace socks shivered against the cool breeze but now I was sailing through the air like a bird.

'Look everyone, I'm doing it. Quick!' I shouted back towards the house. The swing was situated just outside the backdoor, so everyone heard.

'I'm doing it! I'm doing it all on my own. I'm swinging all by myself!' I called.

Even though the house was bursting with both adults and children, my Auntie Kathy came out first followed closely behind by Mum and Nanny Rose. Soon, all three were cheering me on.

'Clever girl, Hayley,' Nana grinned, wiping her fingers against the tea towel which she'd tucked into the top of her skirt. She lifted her hands and clapped wildly.

'Look Steve, Hayley's swinging all by herself!' Nanny Rose called to Dad.

Moments later he appeared and grinned as he watched. Soon quite a crowd had built up as extended family members queued along the back of Nanny Rose's house to watch me on the swing. I felt proud – proud that I'd finally managed to do it after months of trying – but most of all, I was proud that everyone had seen. In fact, I was so pleased with myself that I stayed on the swing until Nana called us inside for Sunday dinner. As usual, the house was a hive of activity, like a busy ship, with Nanny Rose at the helm.

'You take the plates,' I heard her say as I ran in through the door. I turned to the side as she handed a stack of them over to my aunt. 'Mind now,' she warned, as though my aunt was still a child, 'they're a little hot.'

Auntie Kathy nodded and dutifully lined them up along the kitchen worktop, counting them out as she went – seven plates for seven hungry grandchildren.

'Bert, Bert,' Nana called to my granddad, who was snoozing in his armchair. 'The lamb needs carving. Hurry up, the kids are hungry.'

Granddad Bert peeled himself up out of the chair and strolled over to the kitchen. Seconds later, I heard the tell-tale whizz of the electric carving knife as it slid and buzzed its way through the huge succulent meat joint. The delicious aroma of lamb filled the air and made my stomach ache with hunger. I went straight over to the sink to wash my hands with my sister Lauren and our five cousins. We were all starving.

My baby sister Zara was asleep in her pushchair, tucked away in a corner of the dining room. I ran past her and took my usual place at the table. The crisp white cloth had been ironed to within an inch of its life. It was so flat that you could've easily turned a penny on its edge and rolled it clean across the cloth without it faltering. Silver cutlery had been polished and was sparkling, positioned in neat little lines for each child. The knives shone like small mirrors as they reflected the sunlight peeking in through the large back window. Everything was so clean, just how Nanny Rose liked it. Even though there were twice as many adults as kids, Nana insisted her grandchildren sat down to eat first. Every Sunday, everyone from the family including aunts, uncles and cousins would congregate at Nanny Rose's house. Sunday wasn't Sunday if we didn't go to Nanny Rose's.

Rose was my dad's mother but she was also the beating heart of the family. She was a tall woman, standing at 5 feet 8 inches in stocking feet so, to a young child like me, she looked like a giant. Every Sunday she wore the same thing, a loose navy skirt and a white top, but she always kept her trademark white tea-towel tucked into the waistband of her skirt. She also kept a paper tissue, which she folded neatly between her wrist and her chunky gold bangle, in case of emergencies. Sometimes, when the heat of the kitchen became too much, she'd use it to dab her forehead. Nana had a passion for gold jewellery – the chunkier the better. I'd once been told she was the granddaughter of a Romany gypsy. Afterwards I'd spend hours picturing her as a little girl, travelling from town to town, sitting on a horse-drawn caravan selling pegs and lace. With her mystical features, short black curly hair, olive skin and her love of trinkets and crystal, Nanny Rose was the most fascinating woman I knew. Her small home was an absolute treasure trove to a four-year-old girl like me and I'd sit for hours, wide-eyed, staring into tall glass cabinets, mesmerised by all the pretty things inside. Everything was so clean and beautiful and although it was cluttered, everything had its place. From the flawless porcelain dolls and bone china figures, to the miniature Shire horse frozen in time, pulling an ornamental wooden cart along the hearth of the fireplace.

Nanny Rose lived with Granddad Bert in a three-bedroom terraced house in Tooting, London. From the outside, the house looked exactly the same as the other red-brick terraces in the street but once you pushed open the front door, it was like stepping into another world. Like a secret cave buried in a grey and colourless council estate, her home was filled with constant wonder. Plush velvet-covered sofas nestled for space against side tables adorned with ornate lamps bearing heavy tasselled shades. When they were switched off and the sunlight shone in through the window, the shades would cast eerie spiderlike shadows against the wall. Even the TV was boxed away inside a big mahogany cabinet. Once the doors were shut, you wouldn't have even known there was a TV in the room. But it was always on when we were in the house. My sister Lauren and I would sit in front of it all day with the doors flung wide open, watching old Mickey Mouse videos on Granddad's new VHS video recorder. When we weren't perched in front of the telly, we'd be outside picking apples from the tree to help make one of Nanny Rose's legendary apple pies. The tree sat neatly behind the swing at the side of the house, but it was so huge that it shadowed much of the garden because it'd been there for years.

One day, Lauren and I were busy collecting apples. I glanced down at the one in my hand. It was the brightest and prettiest green I'd ever seen, exactly the same colour as freshly mown grass. I held it up to my nose to take a sniff. It smelled so delicious that I felt the urge to take a bite. Licking my lips in anticipation, I opened my mouth and allowed my teeth to crunch into it but as soon as the juice ran inside I called out in horror. My whole body shuddered as the sour acid hit my tongue with a start. It was so tart that, for a moment, I thought I'd bitten straight into a lemon. It was the worst apple I'd ever tasted! I'd made such a racket, coughing and spluttering, that Nanny Rose came dashing over to see what was wrong. As soon as she saw my screwed up face and the half-eaten apple in my hand she burst out laughing.

'No, Hayley,' she giggled, clutching a hand against her chest. 'You can't eat them like that, they're cooking apples. They'll give you bellyache!'

I scrunched up my nose. It didn't make sense. They looked just like normal apples, only a little bigger.

'But they always taste so lovely when you put them in the pie,' I said looking suspiciously at the offending piece of fruit in my hand.

'That's because I put lots of sugar in when I cook them.'

Suddenly the penny dropped. I thought about all the times I'd stood on a chair at the side of the cooker helping out. She was right; Nanny Rose always added a big bowl of sugar to the mixture because sometimes she let me help pour it in. I looked back at the bitter apple. It didn't look as nice as before – my teeth had left small crimp marks along the edge and the fluffy whiteness inside had started to turn a horrible yellowy brown. I stepped back and dropped it to the ground. The bitter juice had left a nasty taste in my mouth. Nanny Rose knelt down at the side of me and took my hand in hers.

'Hayley, if you want something to taste nice then you have to put the effort in – you have to wait.'

Lauren appeared from the other side of the tree and started to laugh when she saw what I'd done. I felt silly. I should've known they were cooking apples, that's why we only picked them when Nanny Rose was baking. I pulled a face. The taste was still there so Nana took me to get a glass of water to wash it away.

'Better?' She asked, taking the beaker from my hand.

I nodded and ran back to the tree. The sun was high in the sky as Lauren and I spent the next hour collecting enough fruit to fill a dozen pies. With our basket full, we headed back inside to find Nana. She was so delighted that she pulled me over into her arms to give me a big hug.

'These are just perfect!'

I buried my head deep into her waist and wrapped my tiny arms around her; the tea towel smelled so good that I could almost taste the apple pie.

'Right, first one to wash all their apples gets to lick the spoon from the stewing apples pan!'

I grinned and picked up some apples. I loved Nana because she always made everything so much fun.

During the holidays, Lauren and I would spend long summer days at her house. There was never a dull moment because we were always playing with the other kids who lived on the council estate. Although I was the youngest, I always got to join in with the older kids' games. My favourite was

'Knock Down Ginger', where a group of us would tap on a random front door and run away as fast as we could. Sometimes I would laugh so hard, it'd make me feel sick. If there were enough of us then we'd have an impromptu game of 'British Bulldog', where everyone would line up and charge at one another. Somehow, someone would always end up on the floor, dirty and with scuffed knees, but it didn't matter because there were always plenty of kids to pick them back up again. Despite our best efforts, Lauren and I were never dressed quite right for the occasion. Instead of jeans, Mum insisted we wore beautiful lace dresses with delicate lace socks and ballet pumps. She'd brush, curl and pin up my hair but it never stayed that way for long. As soon as she'd left for work, I'd be down the bottom of Nana's garden or out in the alleyway, getting filthy, playing rough and tumble with the other kids. Some days, Lauren and I would sit quietly at the bottom of the garden near the shed but we wouldn't do girly things. Instead, we'd sit and line up snails so we could race them along the concrete slabs next to the back gate. It was dark and damp down the bottom of the garden and we'd always find lots of snails creeping about in the hedgerow.

'Hey, you moved your snail too far forward, move it back,' Lauren said pointing straight at my best racer.

I huffed and rolled my eyes. Lauren was a whole year older, so she saw it as her job to be in charge. We fought like most sisters but deep down, I loved her deeply. Sometimes, when Mum or Dad called to pick us up at the end of the day we'd be absolutely filthy but our smiles said it all. It didn't matter that our pretty dresses were muddy, our knees scraped or our ballet pumps wet from puddles because to have proper fun you had to get a little messy. We were typical kids.

During the summer months, we'd go and stay with Nanny Rose and Granddad Bert at Camber Sands, where they owned a chalet by the sea. Mum and Dad would come along too. I've many happy memories of playing badminton on the beach with Granddad, his trousers rolled up at the ankles, or sitting with Dad, building sandcastles on the shoreline. Only one person would be missing, Nanny Rose. She'd be back at the chalet, tucked up in the kitchen, her favourite room. In fact, she wore her famous white tea towel so much I was convinced it was actually sewn onto the front of her clothes. Even to this day, whenever I picture her, she's still wearing that same tea towel.

Nana was the eternal cook and her legendary Sunday dinners became the cement holding our family together. We were a complete unit – a happy family – and it glowed from each and every one of us. The only thing I hated was the vegetables. To me, they just got in the way of the meat. Other nanas would've been stricter but not Nanny Rose. Instead, when my parents weren't looking, she'd slyly slip a bottle of ketchup onto the table so that I could smother my peas and carrots with it. My plate was always slices of meat and huge red tomato mounds where vegetables had once been. The ketchup made them easier to swallow because at least then I didn't have to taste them.

Nanny Rose was a strict Catholic. One afternoon, Dad strolled into her house with Uncle David. The men had been drinking down the pub and were tucking heartily into a couple of meat pies but when Nanny Rose spotted them she went mad. It was Good Friday, and she was cooking fish and chips because she believed Good Friday and Ash Wednesdays were days of abstinence, not for meat pies!

'Get out of my house with that meat!' she screamed, snatching the tea towel from her waistband, whipping them with it.

'You can't eat meat today, it's Good Friday and we're having fish!'

At first, they thought she was joking but Nanny Rose was furious and their laughter only served to infuriate her even more.

'I said, get out, get out!' she wailed like a demented banshee as she took another swipe at them. 'And take your bloody meat pies with you!'

Dad and Uncle David ran towards the backdoor but she didn't stop chasing them until she'd run them clean out into the back garden. She jubilantly slammed the door behind them, calmly tucked her towel back in the waistband of her skirt and went back to preparing the food.

'Meat pies, in my house!' She tutted as she turned towards the cooker.

In the end, we all had fish for supper but Dad and Uncle David were forced to eat their contraband pies outside, underneath the street lamp.

Granddad Bert had a sweet tooth but also a very deep pocket. As soon as he heard the jingle of the ice cream van, he'd dig for change and send us to fetch ice creams. We always chose screwballs because they were our favourite – the chewing gum at the bottom was like having two puddings in one. But after a while, Granddad realised just how much our treats were costing him so he hit on a novel idea.

'When you've finished your ice creams, pop the plastic containers in there.' He said, pointing over towards the kitchen sink.

'Why?' I asked. I was perched on a chair in the kitchen but it was high off the ground and my legs were swinging beneath me like a pendulum.

'Because,' he announced, 'from now on, we're going to make our own screwballs.'

And we did. In fact, our homemade screwballs tasted even better than the ones from the ice cream van because we got to choose our favourite colour chewing gum. Granddad Bert wasn't tight but, with so many grandchildren, making homemade screwballs also made sound financial sense. It kept us all busy on long and wet afternoons as we spent ages scooping ice cream from endless tubs, filling up the freezer. Whatever we did at Nanny Rose's house, we always had fun, until the day that everything changed.

Lauren and I were due to go to a car boot sale in the middle of Tooting, with Nanny Rose and Auntie Tina. As soon as we arrived at Nana's house I ran into the kitchen to say hello but she wasn't there. I dashed from one room to another until I found her, pale and quiet, sitting in the front room in an armchair. It was odd to see her sitting down because usually she was far too busy looking after everyone. Although the adults had followed me into the room, no one said a word about Nana being sat down. Mum left for work and Auntie Tina wheeled something through the door – it was a wheelchair – Nanny Rose's wheelchair. I felt uneasy because I knew it meant something was wrong with her. I started to worry.

*Why did Nana need a wheelchair, she'd never had one before?*

It felt odd, walking along the path with Nanny Rose because, up until that point, she'd been the strongest woman

I knew, but now there she was, slumped inside the wheelchair as if she was broken. I tried not to fret; there must be a good reason for it.

*Maybe she was just tired? Yes, that was it. Nana was just tired. She'd soon be up on her feet again.*

As Auntie Tina pushed her along, I tried to think of the positives. A wheelchair was a novelty – it also meant a free ride on Nanny Rose's knee. But my cousin Kerry was the smallest so she got to go first. Kerry had been born prematurely and was small for her age. My aunt had said that Kerry was so small at birth that she'd even made it into the *Guinness Book of World Records*. Even though we were a similar age, my cousin was as petite and fragile as one of Nanny Rose's porcelain dolls. But now I was annoyed because Kerry was hogging the treat for herself.

'When's it going to be my turn?' I complained at the side of the chair.

It was taking too long to walk to the car boot sale and the back of my legs were aching.

'Soon,' Nanny Rose whispered pulling me close. She winked at me to let me know that it was alright, she'd sort something out.

But another five minutes had passed and I'd still not had my turn. In protest I stopped dead in my tracks and folded my arms angrily across my chest.

'It's not fair!' I huffed.

Nanny Rose chuckled. It was good to see her laugh because I'd been so worried about her and the chair. She uncurled her hands from Kerry's waist and asked her to jump off because now it was my turn. I grinned as she pulled me up into prime position.

'Better?' she whispered in my ear.

'Yes,' I nodded.

And it was, because everything was better when I was with Nanny Rose. I loved being up there because it felt great to be sat on the knee of the most important person. I shut my eyes as the wheelchair rolled along the path and imagined being on a fairground ride. I felt so safe and secure that I never wanted to climb down again. All too soon we reached the car park of the car boot sale. The place was packed with what seemed like hundreds of people milling around looking through other people's knick knacks. Nanny Rose called it all rubbish but she still bought us all an A3 colouring board. There were lots of different pictures to choose from but mine had a picture of a bunny. I couldn't wait to get back to Nana's house and make a start on it but she wanted to have another look round so we did a second circuit of the boot fair. I thought how odd it was, selling off little pieces of your life to strangers. I could never imagine Nana parting with her treasures like that. My Nan spent the whole time sitting, smiling away in her chair but deep down I knew something was wrong. Something had changed overnight. It wasn't something I could see, touch or taste but something was there and I knew that 'something' was slowly taking my Nanny Rose away from me.

The next time we visited her house, Nana was upstairs resting in bed.

'Is she tired?' I asked Mum, my face crumpled with concern.

She glanced down at me but I could tell she didn't know what to say. Instead she just nodded. As she did, Dad turned his face away as though he was upset about something.

'Why don't we go and say hello to her?' Mum suggested brightly.

Lauren and I dashed through to the hallway, flung our coats over the banister, and ran straight upstairs to Nana's bedroom. As soon as we entered, my eyes widened. Nanny Rose looked even paler than I'd remembered. Now she had dark purplish rings underneath her eyes. But as soon as she saw us, those same eyes shone with love as she stretched out her arms in welcome.

'Well, don't just stand there,' she called, 'come and give your Nanny Rose a kiss.'

We instinctively ran over to her but as I wrapped my tiny arms around her, I was amazed at just how far they stretched around her back. I felt the bumps of the bones underneath her skin – as thin and fragile as a baby bird – she looked and felt different.

'That's enough girls,' Mum said after a few moments. 'We don't want to tire Nanny Rose out now, do we?'

Nan smiled and rested her head back on the two huge pillows propped beneath her. Mum gently guided us away towards the door but something made me turn back and wave.

'Bye,' I whispered.

Nanny Rose looked up and smiled but she suddenly looked old, as if a light had gone out inside her. Her skin was paper thin, almost translucent, and her face grey and haunted. I didn't want to leave her there, all alone in her bedroom, but Mum insisted Nana needed to rest. However, before we left, I popped back upstairs to say goodbye properly. Nanny Rose gave me and Lauren lots of kisses but, this time, it was Mum who looked upset. It unnerved me. Later that night I tried to sleep but I couldn't shake off the uneasy feeling or rid myself of the knot twisting inside the pit of my stomach. Something was wrong. The following Sunday, I expected to see Nanny Rose back in her usual spot in the kitchen.

*She'd had lots of sleep; surely she must feel better by now?*

But by the time we arrived, it was Granddad Bert doing all the cooking. He looked odd and out of place standing next to Nanny Rose's cooker. There were a dozen aunts and uncles fussing around him, laying the table and helping to serve dinner, but Granddad looked as helpless and as lost as a small boy. As usual, the children sat down to eat first but when it came to the adults there was one empty space at the table – the most important person was missing. With each Sunday that passed, so the same pattern followed until I almost became used to the space at the table where Nana had once sat. Instead, my beautiful Nanny Rose withered away upstairs until one day, I never saw her again. At first, I didn't understand what had happened. I wanted to know why the adults looked so upset and why some were crying but no one would tell me. In sheer desperation, I turned to my older cousin.

'Why's everyone upset? Where's Nana?'

I begged her to tell but she was frightened she'd get into trouble.

'I'm not allowed to.' She replied. 'Besides, it's so sad that if I did tell you, you'd cry and everyone would know it was me who'd told you.'

'But I won't.' I vowed, crossing my heart with my fingers. 'I won't cry, promise.'

'Promise?'

I nodded my head just to keep her happy. My cousin dramatically checked over each shoulder and then behind her to make sure no one else was listening.

'Nanny Rose got burnt!' She said her eyes wide with horror.

'Burnt!' I gasped.

My hand automatically shot straight up to my mouth to try and stop my shocked cries from escaping. She was lying, she had to be. Tears pricked at the back of my eyes, I willed them to go away but it was useless because soon they came thick and fast, until they spilled out and down my cheeks.

'Shush!' she hissed, putting her finger to her mouth. 'You can't cry, you promised!'

'I'm sorry,' I said wiping away my tears with the back on my sleeve. 'Anyway, I don't care. Not really.'

It was a lie because crying was all I wanted to do. I wanted to scream and shout. I wanted to wail and howl because my beautiful Nanny Rose had gone and now, life would never be the same. My cousin was so annoyed that she stormed out of the room and that's when I really broke down. Once I'd started, I couldn't stop. In the end, Auntie Sue passed by the doorway and caught me sobbing in the corner.

'It's Nanny Rose,' I wept, 'I know she's gone, forever.'

Auntie Sue tried her best to console me.

'It's true Hayley,' she said taking my hand, 'but she's with the angels now. They'll look after her.'

Later that night, I looked out of my bedroom window and up towards the blackened sky trying to picture Nanny Rose. It made me feel a little better to think of her with the angels but try as I might, I couldn't imagine anyone else looking after her because that was her job. It was selfish but I didn't want her up in heaven where I couldn't see her, I wanted her back down on earth with me. Overnight, my idyllic childhood had been ripped to pieces because, after that day, nothing was ever the same again. Granddad Bert still cooked Sunday dinner for us all but it was as though everyone had lost their appetite.

Without Nanny Rose, I couldn't even stomach it anymore. I was only five years old, but her passing left a huge gaping hole in my life and it frightened me. The thought that someone as strong as my Nana could be there one minute and gone the next was so utterly terrifying.

It wasn't until many years later that I learned she'd lost her life to breast cancer. The pain I feel today is still as raw as it was back then. Up until that point, losing Nanny Rose had been the biggest thing to happen to me and her death had a profound and lasting effect because I loved her so much. Her death made me doubt everything because if something could take her away, then surely no one was safe? It triggered a deep-rooted fear which made me question everything. When I was alone I'd sit there and worry about everything and everyone. I didn't realise it then but my life would never be the same again.

## CHAPTER 2

# *JUMPING THE FISHPOND*

DAD'S FISHPOND WAS big, around ten feet long and built in the shape of a figure of eight. In the narrowest part it measured four feet across – far too wide for a small child like me to step or jump over – and it was full of Koi carp. There were different coloured fish, from silver and orange through to the deepest blue-black. If I looked hard enough I'd catch a glimpse of their scales as they glinted against the light. Although I was happy to look from a safe distance I didn't want to get too close because I was frightened of them. I didn't like the way the big ones swished quickly through the water. I hated the slime of the pond and the way the carp would quickly change direction. I didn't like the speed of them, the unpredictability, but most of all, I didn't like their huge, dead-looking glassy eyes and open mouths which surfaced every time they popped up for air. In short, Dad's fish terrified me.

'Why are you so frightened of them Hales?' he asked one afternoon as I skirted warily around the edge of the pond.

Dad was shaking in pellet feed. The round, hard shapes landed on top of the water before slowly bobbing and sinking down into the murky depths below. The thought of all those hungry fish made my stomach turn. To me, my father's Koi carp looked as dangerous and frightening as sharks in the sea.

'I'm frightened they'll bite my toes off,' I confided.

Dad stifled a giggle but he didn't quite laugh because he knew it'd upset me. This was a real fear.

'But they're just fish Hales. They won't hurt you.'

I didn't believe him. Instead, I suffered nightmares where Dad's Koi carp would eat my toes. I was so frightened that my dreams would jolt me awake in the middle of the night. The fishpond held every fear I had. But my fears also made me a little curious and, every time I was in the garden, I'd dare myself to edge a little closer to see if I could see the 'sharks'. But I never got too close in case one jumped out of the water and bit me on the nose!

At the time, we lived in a five bedroom semi-detached house in Balham, London. There was me, Lauren, Zara, Mum and Dad and Nanny Linda, Mum's mother, who lived with us. After Nanny Rose's death, I often found myself watching Nanny Linda because I was worried she'd get sick and die. Thankfully, she was as fit as a fiddle. Nanny Linda had lived with us for as long as I could remember. Her husband, Granddad Guy, had passed away when I was just a baby so I didn't remember him. Instead, Nanny Linda told me stories from the past which I used to fill in the blanks. She told me how one day Granddad Guy had fallen down right in front of her. He suffered from something called emphysema – a horrible word that stuck inside my head. It was an illness which meant he couldn't breathe properly.

'He just fell on the floor,' Nanny Linda recalled, her eyes watering with tears.

I was sitting on the edge of her bed, hanging onto her every word.

'What did you do?' I gasped.

'I was so scared Hayley, that I sort of froze to the spot. It was your Uncle Duncan who got down and gave him mouth to mouth. He tried to get him breathing again...' Her voice trailed off to a whisper as she tried to compose herself.

I pictured my uncle breathing into Granddad's mouth, trying to bring him back to life for my lovely nana.

'But it was no good,' she said wandering over towards her bedroom window. 'He died right there and then.'

Nanny Linda said Granddad Guy had been the love of her life. She loved him so much that she never, ever wanted to be parted from him. That's why she kept his ashes in a tub inside a special cupboard in her bedroom.

'It's so we can be buried together,' she explained.

When Granddad died, my parents insisted Nanny Linda come to live with us. In many ways, she became my second mother. She helped look after me and my two sisters when Mum and Dad were at work. I often wondered why Nanny Linda never remarried but she insisted it was because no one could ever take Granddad's place. It was as if by remarrying, she'd somehow be unfaithful to him. For Nanny Linda, marriage was for life.

Our back garden was large with a cubed-shaped blue play slide. Dad's fishpond sat to the side in pride of place. In many ways it was his jewel in the crown and he'd spend hours cleaning it out, checking on his dozens of fish. Lauren and I would fall about laughing every time Dad cleaned out the pond because he'd emerge from the house dressed in a pair of high-fitting khaki-coloured rubber waders. We'd squeal with laughter because the rubber came right up to his waist and made it look as though he was wearing a skirt. Then in he'd climb, wearing his rubber 'skirt', wading through the water like a professional fisherman, holding a net in his hand. I watched him from the slide because secretly, I was terrified he'd topple over and fall in and the vicious fish would eat him up. They never did of course, but the fear was real. I watched from afar until one day when everything changed. I still can't recall how it started or why I even did it, but something told me to climb up onto the raised platform and tip-toe along the edge of the pond. It was as though there was a voice inside me, a braver Hayley willing me on to see if I'd do it. Soon, the urge was so strong that I couldn't stop myself. As I took my first tentative steps, I stole a breath. The water looked inky black and as sinister as I'd imagined. The more I looked down, the more I saw – the odd flash of silver and orange glinting like tiny torches against the beams of daylight. It was so sunny I could even make out Dad's biggest fish, which were a strange mixture of bluish grey and black. They scared me most because they were huge, almost two feet long. They were scarier than the others because they were so dark that they were virtually invisible. The sort who'd sneak up on you when you least expected and take a bite out of you. The thought of the fish terrified me. I jumped down from the edge – I'd done enough for today.

Days later, I was at it again, only this time the voice which had told me to walk along the edge of the pond was now daring me to go one step further – this time I had to jump it.

My heart was thudding as I climbed back up onto the edge. I held a hand against my mouth as I surveyed the size of it. I knew I couldn't jump the length because it was far too long but the width was so much narrower. Even though it was wider than I was tall, I knew I was good at jumping so I told myself I could do it – I could jump the fishpond! As the idea danced around inside my head I remembered the scary fish inside.

*What if they chomped at my fingers and toes?*

The thought of them made me feel sick but there was something else – I couldn't swim. It should've been enough to make me walk away but something kept me there. The compulsion to jump over the water had quite literally glued my feet to the spot until it was all I could think of. My mind raced with random thoughts as they whizzed and whirred inside my head.

*If I jumped the fishpond then everyone would be really pleased. If I jumped the pond and made it to the other side then maybe bad things wouldn't happen and everyone would stay safe?*

I knew it was crazy, even at five years old, but somehow because it was so crazy it also seemed to make perfect sense. In order to stop awful things from happening, I'd have to put myself at risk because at least that way nothing awful would happen to my family again.

I glanced up and around me. Lauren was playing happily in the bottom corner of the garden near the slide. The pond beckoned me until I forgot all about my sister and focused on what I had to do. I wandered around the edge until I was standing at the narrowest part – the pinched-in bit of the figure of eight. If I was going to clear it then I'd have to jump that part, otherwise I'd fall in.

*But what if I didn't make it? What if the horrible sharks gobbled me up? What if I drowned?*

I stole a breath. By now, panic had set in and my heart was racing as I tried to shake the negative thoughts from my head. The doubts were still there, niggling away at the back of my brain like the fish nibbling at my toes, but I could do this and I had to, to keep my family safe. I shuddered because I was too scared to jump and too scared not to. If I didn't jump then bad things would happen, like Nanny Rose dying, and it'd all be my fault. Soon, the urge was so strong that I couldn't contain it any longer.

*Imagine how pleased everyone would be? Imagine how clever they'd think I was?*

I thought back to the day on Nanny Rose's swing, when everything was perfect and everyone was well. I wanted, *no, I needed*, everyone to tell me how well I'd done. I wanted them all to see, but only when I'd cleared it, then they'd all be happy.

I glanced over at Lauren. Her head was bowed as though she was in deep thought, playing in her own imaginary world yet, there I was, about to take the biggest jump of my life. My eyes darted over towards the back of the house. Mum and Nanny Linda were busy inside. I could see Nana; she was ironing in the kitchen. Mum was cleaning the house; I spotted her head as she walked inside the kitchen to pick up something. I waited until she'd moved away from the window and then I knew it was time.

*I can do this,* the voice inside my head urged.

It was right, I could do this and I had to do it now. Gritting my teeth, I took a few steps back, enough to take a running jump. I screwed my eyes up tight so that I wouldn't see the water and took an extra deep breath for courage. I gulped in so much air that my lungs felt fit to burst. When I was sure I couldn't breathe in any more I ran towards the pool at full pelt. Like a steam train – nothing, no one, could stop me. My feet lifted up and left the safety of the paving slabs. Soon I was falling against thin air, my hands, arms and legs splaying against nothingness. The cold water enveloped me almost immediately and brought me back into the moment. It choked me as it slipped up inside my nose and mouth, working its way like a snake down into my lungs, before stealing my breath. I instinctively put out my arms to stop myself from sinking deeper, but as I did thin webs of green slime slipped through my fingers. I heard the muffled and distorted sound of voices coming from above and saw dark shadows silhouetted against the sunlight. People were frantically looking down at me, watching me sink. I don't remember who dragged me out but I do remember the almighty telling off I got from Mum.

'Why did you do that, you silly girl? You could've drowned!' she screeched, as I choked and spluttered in front of her.

The taste in my mouth was vile, even worse than the sour apple. I coughed and spat something out – putrid green water splashed against the floor by my feet. The look and taste of it made me want to retch and I started to shake.

'What's wrong with you?' Mum was screaming. 'You could've died! Why did you do it, tell me why you did it, Hayley?'

Three pairs of eyes looked straight at me as Nanny Linda, Mum and Lauren waited for an answer I didn't have.

'I fell in,' I lied.

Mum shook her head in disbelief.

'Well, thank God we saw you when we did, otherwise who knows what could've happened!'

She was so angry that she was shaking too.

'You could've drowned!'

*How could I tell her that I hadn't fallen in, that it hadn't been an accident – that the real reason I'd ended up in the water was because I needed to jump the pond?*

It took a while, but eventually Mum calmed down. To be honest, I think I'd frightened her almost as much as I had myself. Thankfully, I managed to escape without any shark bites that day and, other than a sore throat from swallowing too much water and a bit of green slime which had stained my skin; it was nothing a hot bath and good scrub wouldn't sort out. Despite my near-death experience, soon I was as good as new. It spurred me on to have another go.

The next time I tried to jump the pond it was a weekend. Dad had been in and out of the house all day doing various bits of DIY, so I waited until he'd nipped back inside before I took a running jump.

*This time I'll clear it, I just know I will,* the voice inside my head convinced me. It repeated it over and over, like a mantra.

But I didn't clear it; in fact, I didn't come anywhere close but landed right in the middle and sank straight to the bottom like a stone. Dad saw me and ran across the garden to fish me out.

'What are you doing, Hayley?' he gasped, his voice rising with panic. 'You shouldn't go near the pond, you could've drowned!'

But the thought of dying didn't deter me because I needed to do this, to keep everyone safe. If anything, trying to prove that I could and would clear it seemed to make it more of a challenge. The third time I jumped the pond was the most upsetting of all. That afternoon, I'd been invited to a boy's party in the neighbourhood. Mum had been out and bought me a brand new dress. I loved my party dress; it was all white with a big swishy skirt and lots of girly frills. It was absolutely perfect. Mum had spent ages styling my hair until it was curled at the sides and pinned up on top with a big bow. Even my socks had lace and frills and my shoes were black and shiny. I was all ready for my party. As I stood inside the kitchen waiting for Mum, I twisted my feet so that I could admire my shoes. As I did, I noticed the fishpond out of the corner of my eye. It was still there, calling to me through the window, urging me to give it just one more try. I was lovely and clean and all ready to go but something told me to open up the backdoor and wander over towards the pond.

*Maybe my smart new clothes would help? Maybe they'd give me extra power?*

I needed to find out. I'd never cleared it before but today, something told me it would be different. This time, I'd jump it in one go.

Mum hadn't noticed me slip out into the garden because she was busy talking to Nanny Linda. As I stood at the edge of the pond, I glanced back at the house. The coast was clear.

The crazy paving felt uneven beneath my feet and the water in the pond was as dark and unwelcoming as I remembered. It was a hot day and the stench rising from it made me recoil but the sun was shining high in a virtually cloud-free sky and today felt better and full of hope. Today would be different because today I'd jump the pond.

*This time I'll clear it. This time I'll make it across, I just know it.* The voice convinced me.

I closed my eyes and took the deepest breath I could. Then I began to run. The faster I ran the more I imagined the happy faces, cheers and applause as I landed safely on the other side. My party dress would still be immaculate and I'd be hailed a hero – Hayley the hero. Mum and Dad would be so pleased because they wouldn't have to worry about me not being able to swim anymore. Once I'd jumped the pond everything would be great. As I ran I felt my feet leave the earth as they sailed and then scrambled through the air.

*Almost there,* the voice told me, *I was almost at the other side. This time I'd make it. This time everything would be better.*

The coldness of the water slapped me sharply like a hand across my face. A huge blanket of water whooshed over the top of my head swallowing me whole. Coldness froze against my skin making it numb, as my arms tangled against watery cobwebs. Suddenly, the whip of something against my back caused me to panic.

*It was them; the fish were coming to get me!*

My heart pounded as I struggled to untangle both my fingers and hair from the weeds. But the more I struggled, the more they seemed to pull me under like swirling green hands dragging me to my death. I was simply terrified.

*What if no one had seen? What if no one came to my rescue? What if I drowned and died at the bottom of the pond?*

My fingers fumbled around, trying to hold onto something, anything. I realised I didn't want to die. I was only five. I just wanted everything to be back how it was. I imagined myself standing above, at the side of the water, dressed in my pristine party dress.

*What if I never saw my parents or Nanny Linda ever again?*
My stomach lurched.

*What if I landed at the bottom of the pond and the fish ate me, chewing me up into small pieces? No one would ever find me.*

My heart pounded with fear. Suddenly, a distant voice sounded above. My eyes felt fuzzy as I tried to look through the dirty water. It was hard but I looked up towards the light and that's when I saw a blurred and horrified face peering straight down at me. She was mostly shadow but I knew immediately who it was – my sister Lauren.

'Mum, quick! Hayley's in the pond again!' Her voice sounded muffled and distorted through the thickness of the water.

Another figure appeared and then a hand reached down. It grabbed the front of my dress and I felt a frantic tug and then relief at the sensation of being pulled upwards, towards the light. As soon as I reached the surface I gasped for air. The hand had belonged to Mum and now she was standing there and she was absolutely furious.

'For God's sake Hayley!' she screamed. 'Look at the state of you, your dress is ruined!'

I looked down; it was stained green from the slime and dirty water. Mum was right, everything was ruined. I'd ruined everything.

'In fact, forget it; you can't go to the party.'

The rescue, the fresh air, but more importantly, the impact of what I'd just done hit me and I promptly burst into tears. Mum was trembling with both fear and anger as I dripped in front of her. Nanny Linda always tried her best to keep the peace but even she couldn't hold her tongue when she saw me and came running over.

'Oh balls! Has she been in the bloody fishpond again?' she asked, clamping her hand over her mouth in horror.

It seemed to make Mum even worse.

'Your dress is ruined! You'll never be able to wear it ever again.' She shouted. 'I may as well put it all straight in the bin. Why did you do it? You could have drowned, you silly girl. You can't swim! Tell me, tell me why you did it?'

But the problem was I didn't know. Instead, I wept because I'd frightened myself. I was upset because my pretty party dress was ruined but most of all, I cried because I knew I'd worried Mum. But she saw how distraught I was and softened a little.

'It's okay,' she said looking over at Nanny Linda. 'You can go to the party. But,' she said raising a finger as if to make a point, 'you never, ever go near the pond again. Agreed?'

I nodded my head.

'Go on then,' she said pointing towards the house. 'You'll have to get washed and, as for your dress, well, that'll have to go straight in the bin.'

I didn't look at Mum or Nanny Linda because I felt ashamed. Ashamed of what I'd done. The worst part was I didn't even know why I'd done it. I turned and walked sadly back towards the house. I'd ruined everything. My dress, socks and shoes were soaked and my hair was a tangled mess of knotted, wet curls and blanket weed. I shivered with shock and cold as I lifted my shoulder and sniffed it – I stunk to high heaven and it was my fault. I was devastated about my party dress because it'd been the prettiest one in the shop and now I'd never get the chance to wear it again.

Nanny Linda helped scrub me clean in the bath but as much as she loved me, I could see her wondering exactly the same thing as Mum.

*What was wrong with Hayley?*

'You're a bloody mare, you are!' she said, shaking her head in despair as she scrubbed my neck and back with the soapy sponge.

I was a little late getting to the party and, in the end, I wore an older and much less 'swingy' dress. I was upset because I'd felt so lovely before but now I looked dull and dowdy. Sure enough, Mum threw the dress in the bin. I don't know if she told Dad because nothing else was said but when I returned home I was so distressed that I cried myself to sleep.

*Why did I have to keep jumping the pond and why did I have to keep upsetting them all so much?*

But I didn't know the answer. In my own mind, I was doing it to protect them but how could I tell them that? Just saying it sounded wrong. My urge to jump was so strong that I knew it wouldn't go away until I had.

The next time I jumped the pond, both my parents were at work. Nanny Linda was sitting watching us in the garden. It was a red hot day in the middle of the school holidays. Lauren and I had been messing about with the hosepipe all morning, looping it down the slide so we could slide along a little faster. Nanny Linda was resting in a chair reading a book. She was dressed in a swimsuit and shorts. Every time I walked past her I could smell olive oil because she used it on her skin. We used proper suntan cream but Nanny Linda always used oil. Her family were from Greece, and her dark skin never seemed to burn. She was a petite woman with long, dark hair. At one point it was so long that it almost touched her bum but, as she got older, she cut it until eventually, it ended up in a neat tight perm on the top of her head.

By the afternoon, I felt a little chilled so I changed back into my clothes and I wandered back out into the garden. Nana was sitting with Zara, who was still in her pushchair. The hood was up and she had a hat on to shield her against the sun. I looked across at the pond. It was calling to me again, daring me to jump it. I sat down and tried to think of something else. I needed to forget about the pond. But, try as I might, I just couldn't. The urge was so strong that I rose to my feet. Nana momentarily turned away to fuss over Zara, who was holding a bunch of baby keys in her hands. Nana was rattling them and was so engrossed that she didn't notice me slip away and walk over towards the water. Once again, I shut my eyes and took an almighty jump.

'You bloody mare!' I heard Nana's voice screech from across the garden just as I hit the water.

Once again, I was right at the bottom but as I looked up all I could see was her tiny silhouette against the light above. A hand plunged in and down towards me as Nanny Linda fished me out, choking and stinking. To be honest, I don't think her eyes left me even for a second because she was at the side of the pool as quick as a flash. Everyone knew I couldn't be trusted near water. Everyone knew what I was like, even if they didn't know why I did it. As I stood there dripping wet, I steeled myself for another almighty telling off so I was a little confused when I didn't get one. Instead, Nanny Linda was kind, concerned even.

'What are you like? Well, we better get you cleaned up before your mum sees you. Here,' she said taking my hand, 'Let's pop you in the bath before she gets home.'

My shoes made a horrible squelching sound as I walked along the grass and back towards the house. Dirty green water rose and spilled over the sides of them with every step

I took. I was cold but relieved that Nana wasn't cross with me. I even caught her smiling which baffled me.

'You're a bloody mare, you are!' she chuckled.

I didn't know what the word 'mare' was but it stuck inside my head. For the rest of the day, I wondered what it meant. It wasn't until I was older that I realised she'd meant I was a nightmare. She was right, I was.

'Are you going to tell Mum?' I asked my eyes wide with worry.

'No,' she replied. 'I'm not. Now take those wet clothes off and hop in the bath.'

As I stepped into the bath I turned to face her.

'Whatever you do, don't tell your mum you fell in the fishpond,' she whispered.

I shook my head. I wouldn't tell Mum or anyone else. Lauren had seen of course, but Nana told me not to worry because she'd speak to her. She put a finger to her lips as if it was our secret.

'I won't tell anyone,' she insisted.

And she didn't. Even though I jumped the pond another five times after that day, true to her word, Nanny Linda never told a soul.

## CHAPTER 3

# *FEAR OF EATING OUT*

IT HAD BEEN Dad's idea to take us all out for a meal.

'That'll be nice,' Mum agreed as she sent us upstairs to get changed.

It was a large, traditional family pub which looked just like a country cottage from the outside. It was nice and homely inside with plush red velvet seats, a dark red carpet and lines of neat wooden tables. Pretend candle-style lampshades hung from the walls gently lighting each table booth. The place was packed because it was a Saturday night, but Dad had insisted we go because he wanted to treat us, even Nanny Linda. As soon as we walked in we were herded over to a special rope barrier until a waitress showed us to our table. I was really excited because back then going out for a meal was a pretty expensive thing to do. Moments later, we sat down. The laminated menu felt huge in my hands as my eyes scanned it, trying to read all the stuff. There were lots of things to choose from but I was a typical kid and all I wanted was something plain and simple, so I chose burger and chips. Dad placed our order adding a huge starter platter for everyone to share. As soon as it arrived my eyes widened because it was crammed with everything from chicken wings to potato skins and sour cream – I'd never seen so much food. Mum leaned across the table, picked up mine and Lauren's plates and placed a few things on each. I'd always had a small appetite and the starter filled me up quickly so, when I saw the waitress approach with my main meal I was worried how I'd manage it all.

'Ooh, yours looks good,' Lauren commented as the waitress placed the plate in front of me.

As I stared at it, my stomach cramped and knotted. There were too many chips and the burger was so massive I wondered how I'd eat it all. Just the thought of it inside my mouth made me feel queasy. Picking up a bottle of tomato ketchup, I poured some on my plate but as soon as I picked up my fork, I started to feel really self-conscious, as though everyone inside the pub was watching. I glanced down at my plate. The burger looked nice enough but I was worried how I'd fit it in inside my mouth.

*What if all the insides come spurting out across my chin?* I thought randomly. My body shuddered as the image whirred around inside my head.

*It'd look horrible and disgusting. I'd look disgusting and everyone would see.*

Suddenly, I'd lost my appetite – now I felt sick with nerves. I put my fork down and stole a quick glance.

*Was anyone watching?*

Of course, no one was but it wasn't enough to calm my fear.

*They'll all watch me try to eat this and I'll look really ugly. Everyone here will think how ugly I look.*

I was thankful there wasn't a mirror nearby because I didn't want to catch a glimpse of myself trying to eat. My stomach felt all knotted up inside and my mouth was bone dry. The burger didn't even feel like food anymore, just a huge mountain I'd have to climb. I looked at it but I didn't feel hungry, I just felt frightened.

*The burger is so big that if I put in my mouth, it'll just spill out everywhere.*

My throat seized up as if something was slowly squeezing the life out of me. Panic set in as my pulse began to race. I wiped my hands against my dress, they felt clammy too. I tried not to imagine myself eating but I couldn't help it. I'd look horrible – with my face contorted and greedy – even the thought of it made me feel sick. My breath became shallow and laboured as the room started to swim. The sudden dizziness combined with hot smells from other people's food hit my nostrils and made my stomach turn but I didn't want to say anything because I didn't want to spoil the big night out. Mum looked up, she realised I wasn't eating and asked if something was wrong.

'No,' I lied, straightening up in my seat.

But everything was wrong. I tried to act normal. I picked up my fork and stabbed randomly at a chip but it took all the strength I had just to lift it up towards my mouth. I had to take a bite but something was stopping me, like an invisible force. My eyes anxiously darted around to check if anyone was watching. I expected to find the whole restaurant staring straight back at me, but no one was because they were far too busy chatting and eating. Even though I knew it was crazy, the fear refused to go away. Seconds later, my heart quickened and started to race as I tried my best to take a bite. I had to do it – I had to eat something before someone noticed. I saw Lauren tucking into her dinner and felt envious.

*Why couldn't I be normal like my sister? Why couldn't I just eat my food?*

But the fear was real and it was still there choking me. My heart thumped as bile rose up inside my throat. I tried to breathe as I lifted the burger up towards my mouth. The bread bun felt slippery, hot and greasy between my fingers. Even the smell of it made me want to heave.

*You have to do this, you can't ruin everyone's night.*

As the food drew closer to my face I could feel the heat as steam brushed against my skin. I closed my eyes and tried to focus. Blood whooshed inside my brain and I felt hot and prickly as I forced myself to take a miniscule bite. The bread crushed against my teeth and stuck to the roof of my mouth which made my stomach contract. I knew I was going to be sick. My eyes darted around, looking for something to spit my food into. I saw a red napkin and spat the burger into it.

'I think I'm going to be sick,' I gasped as I ran towards the ladies loo.

Mum dashed after me. I'd just made it to the toilet when I vomited so hard that sick came out of both my nostrils and my mouth.

'Hayley, what's wrong?' Mum asked holding my hair away from my face.

But I couldn't answer. All I knew was I felt worse than I'd ever felt in my entire life. My insides twisted as my stomach muscles heaved. Finally they stopped contracting and the sickness subsided. Mum wrapped an arm around my shoulder.

'Come on, love.'

She turned me towards her and, with a wad of toilet tissue, mopped both my face and hands.

'Here, let's get you over to the sink. You can splash your face with cold water, that'll make you feel better.'

Mum's concern was so genuine that it made me feel worse because deep down, I knew it wasn't the food making me sick, it was me – I'd done it to myself. As the cold water hit my skin, I began to feel better. I caught a glimpse of my reflection in the toilet mirror – my face was pale and pasty. Of course, Mum put the sickness down to a stomach bug, only I knew better. It wasn't a bug or virus making me sick; it was a fear – a fear of eating out in public. Something inside my mind was making me sick. Just like the urge to jump the fishpond, now it was telling me not to eat food because strangers might be watching me. Now I'd been sick, I felt a whole lot better, if not a little confused. These things kept happening to me but I didn't know why. Something had told me not to eat the burger, but to jump the fishpond. It wasn't something I could see or even explain. I couldn't tell anyone what it was because I didn't know myself.

*How could I tell anyone how frightened I felt? How could I expect anyone else to understand?*

'Maybe you were just too full up, maybe you just ate too much,' Mum said as we returned to the table. 'I wouldn't eat anything else, just in case.'

I nodded. She was right; if I didn't eat anything else then I wouldn't be sick. I didn't want to be ill because I didn't want to go home. Despite the food, I enjoyed us all being out together because usually Dad was at work. He was a partner in a printing business in London, which he ran with Uncle

Peter, so he was almost never home. We only ever saw him for a couple of hours each night before we went to bed. Sometimes, it was almost as though he didn't live there at all.

After that day, whenever we went out for something to eat I'd panic every time my meal arrived at the table but I never showed my fear. Instead, I taught myself to hide it. I'd pretend to wipe my mouth with a napkin just so I could secretly spit out the food. On other occasions, I'd eat it only to go straight to the toilet where I'd be violently sick. I never ever made myself sick – I didn't have to – my body was in such a state of panic that it did it for me. But the fear other people were watching me was always there. I'd manage to eat the starter as long as I shared it. I didn't mind food I could pick at; I just couldn't eat a whole dinner to myself. As long as I hid my secret then no one would find out and everything would be fine. No one would know because as soon as I was sick, I always felt better.

Back at home I was able to eat normally; I just felt intimidated in a restaurant. It was as though this new fear had stolen my appetite for food and life. I didn't realise it then, but the fishpond and my new fear of eating in public were the beginnings of something much bigger and it was something which would slowly rule, and all but destroy, my life.

COMING CLEAN
LIVING WITH OCD

## CHAPTER 4

# BREAK-UPS AND MAKEUP

MUM HAD WORKED behind the makeup counter at Selfridges for as long as I could remember but one day she left and started at a new company, doing the accounts. With both parents at work, Nanny Linda stepped in to look after me and my sisters. I didn't mind because to us, Nanny Linda was our second mum. Soon, Mum and Dad were passing like ships in the night. She'd cook Dad's tea and we'd see him for a couple of hours before being packed off to bed. This pattern continued for the best part of a year until one day, Mum had something to tell us.

'Dad's not going to be living here anymore,' she said wringing her hands nervously in her lap. My eyes automatically followed them and I took a sharp breath when I realised she'd already removed her wedding ring.

I looked over at Lauren and Zara but they didn't even flinch. The sad truth was that, despite his best efforts, none of us saw Dad anymore. The business had all but consumed him until it had slowly stolen him away from us. Mum was also busy, wrapped up in her new job. I thought it was sad they'd suddenly stopped loving one another. Even though I thought about it, I never asked Mum any questions, none of us did – we just accepted it. As long as Nanny Linda was still with us, I knew we'd be okay.

In fact, in many ways, Dad leaving had its bonuses, mainly the plush new apartment he moved into. It was part of a huge block of flats in London, but he shared a swimming pool and gardens with the other residents. We visited Dad every other weekend, when we'd get to stay over. I loved it there because we'd spend endless days swimming, laughing and chatting. The swimming pool made me feel like my dad was a millionaire – no one else's dad I knew had a swimming pool.

Back at home everything stayed the same and soon our fractured family became our new way of life. Months later, Mum introduced us to her new boyfriend, a man called Paul. They'd met at work, she told me. Meanwhile, Dad had a girlfriend of his own – a lovely woman called Carol. She was a single mum and pub landlady from Clapham, with two children – a boy and a girl. They were called Joseph and Rachel and I loved spending time with them because they were still so young. Joseph was four years old and a typical boy, boisterous and lots of fun, while Rachel was still a baby.

'Aww, a baby!' I squealed with delight as soon as we met.

I put out my arms to hold Rachel, and Carol let me. It made me feel important, like a miniature mum. Joseph was tiny in comparison to my youngest sister Zara, even though she was only a year older than him. He was so slight that I was able to pick him up and spin him around in my arms.

'Faster, faster!' he giggled until I spun him so fast that we both felt dizzy.

Despite my new family and the fact my parents were both moving on with their lives, my compulsions never left me. My fear of eating out remained but the urge to jump the fishpond was eventually overtaken by another compulsion. I was still only seven years old, but this new obsession would quite literally change my world.

One day, I walked into the bedroom I shared with my elder sister Lauren. We had a big bedroom. It was painted pale green and had a tall wooden bunk bed pressed up against the wall in the right-hand corner. Opposite stood a large dark oak wardrobe which was crammed full of clothes. Take That posters adorned the walls, although Lauren was a much bigger fan than I was. I loved our bedroom but I'd never given it or the things in it a second thought until today. It had been a mundane rainy afternoon with very little to do. I'd been playing downstairs with Lauren and Zara, but as soon as I walked into our bedroom, everything looked wrong – it all seemed so cluttered. The wardrobe was far too big for the corner, even though it had stood there for as long as I could remember, and the bunk bed was too sharp and angular in the right hand side of the room. I shook my head in despair – everything had to be moved. My hands were clammy so I wiped them against the hem of my dress. Even the top of the white chest of drawers looked messy, scattered with hairbrushes, bands and bobbles. Everything needed sorting and I'd be the one to put it all back in order again.

*How could we have let it get into such a state? Why hadn't I noticed before?*

The more I glanced around, the more I saw. My heart

thudded inside my chest as panic gripped me – I couldn't believe I'd been sleeping in such a messy bedroom! It all had to be rearranged and it had to be done now. Pushing the door closed behind me, I looked across at the wardrobe. Besides the bunk bed, it was the largest piece of furniture so it needed moving first. There was just one problem; it was far too heavy for me. I stood back and scratched my head. For a moment I thought about shouting down to Lauren to give me a hand, but I dismissed the idea because she'd only argue and say where everything should go. But I already knew where things had to go and I didn't want anyone messing it up – I'd have to do this alone. Gripping my fingers around the edge of the wood I tried to yank the wardrobe away from the wall and towards me. My knuckles flashed white as I pulled as hard as I could but I realised it was impossible. I stood back; I'd have to think of a better way. The wardrobe wasn't on wheels; it didn't even have 'feet', only a flat base. I knew if I could get enough strength behind it I'd be able to push, rather than pull it along. But first I'd have to create a small gap, small enough to crawl into. I spanned my arms out once more and, using all my might, I gave it a small tug, which caused the wardrobe to shift slightly. It was all the encouragement I needed. I tugged again and again, using small bursts of energy until soon, it had shifted a few feet away from the wall. Squeezing inside the gap, I wedged my back up against the wardrobe and pushed as hard as I could until there was enough room to sit down. Placing my feet flat against the bedroom wall like a human crowbar, I heaved with my back and shoulders. Instead of jarring, the wooden base slid along the smooth carpet like a knife against butter until, ten minutes later, it was exactly where I wanted it to be

– at the other end of the room. I was satisfied because it definitely looked better over there. I considered the bunk bed – it was even heavier than the wardrobe. Placing my feet flat against the wall, I forced my back against it. Using my feet as a guide and my back as the force, I edged it around the room. It was tiring work and it took ages. I was sweating profusely and my thin top was sticking to my skin, but I refused to give up – I *needed* our bedroom to be perfect. After more huffing and puffing, I managed to manoeuvre the bed into a better place. Then I tackled the chest of drawers using the same technique and brute force. With everything in place, I calmly picked up and sorted through the hair bands and bobbles, arranging them into little neat colour-coded piles. I wiped the top of the drawers even though they weren't dusty as cleaning somehow made me feel calmer. Finally, I took a step back and admired my handiwork. A contented smile spread across my face.

*Not bad!* The voice congratulated me.

My pounding heart started to slow and calm. With everything less cluttered and lined up I felt better because where there'd once been mess, now there was order. It'd taken me ages to move it all but the satisfaction I now felt made it worthwhile. A slight draught brushed against my back as the door opened behind me.

'What's going on?' It was Lauren. She gasped and her mouth fell open as she looked around the room. 'Hayley, what have you done?'

'Do you like it?'

'Yes,' she replied. 'It just looks so different.'

'But it looks nice? It looks better?' I offered.

Lauren nodded.

'Yes, it does look better,' Lauren decided, jumping up onto the bed. 'I love it!'

I should've been happy, satisfied that I'd sorted it all out, but I never was. To me, after that day it never looked quite right. There was always something that needed moving. If it looked wrong, then it was. It became an itch I had to scratch and soon I was doing it all the time.

One afternoon, Lauren walked into the bedroom just as I was pushing the last piece of furniture into place, only this time she didn't look happy.

'Mum, Hayley's moving the furniture again!' she hollered.

I shot her a hateful stare.

Mum's footsteps sounded on the stairs and I cursed Lauren for telling. Mum crossed the hallway until there she was, standing right in the middle of the doorway. I'd been caught bang to rights, with my back wedged up against the wardrobe and my feet on the wall.

'Hayley, stop that! You'll hurt yourself!' Mum said.

'Okay,' I replied, but I didn't mean it.

Instead, I waited until she'd gone back downstairs. Once the coast was clear, I moved the rest of the furniture because, by now, I couldn't stop myself. If I didn't move it then I knew something bad would happen and I'd be responsible. Also, I knew just where everything needed to be, no one else did. No one else could make it perfect, and it had to be right otherwise bad things would happen.

But Lauren got fed up with me moving her stuff.

'Stop touching my things,' she snapped one afternoon.

She was protective of her possessions and didn't like me moving the soft toys from her bed. I didn't mind sharing a room as long as I could control where everything went. I even

44

colour co-ordinated our clothes hanging up inside the wardrobe. The more Lauren complained, the more I dreamed of having my own room. Our house was big enough but Nanny Linda had one room and my parents kept another spare for Uncle Roger. He lived in Hong Kong but he often came to London on business and kept all his belongings in the other bedroom.

As the months passed, so the furniture migrated around the bedroom in an endless cycle. In fact, I was so busy moving stuff that I soon forgot about jumping the fishpond until I no longer thought about it at all. Instead, I became consumed with other worries, particularly my appearance. My insecurities occupied every spare moment I had until I constantly fretted and fussed over my looks. I was getting older and, like most girls, judged myself against others in my class. Everything bothered me about my face. My eyes didn't look right – they were too small. I hated my reflection because my eyes always looked wrong, whatever I did to them. I focused in on them and myself until they became my new obsession. I needed to find something to make them look bigger. When Mum worked at Selfridges, she regularly brought home makeup samples which she kept locked inside a vanity box, tucked in a corner of her bedroom. The box was enormous and stood on four metal legs which were so tall they reached up to my waist. Whenever I undid it, it would open out into a cascade of different makeup compartments. One day, I was rifling through these compartments when my fingers stumbled upon something: a tube of thick black mascara. As I rolled it over in the palm of my hand, I knew it was perfect. It was just the thing I needed to emphasise my eyes. My hand was a little shaky and unsure as I coated each lash with the black gooey mixture. Within seconds, my lashes had extended. I was amazed, almost immediately I looked and felt better because my face looked as though someone had drawn on a new and prettier pair of eyes. The more I stared at my reflection, the more something changed inside. My face looked better, it wasn't perfect, but the black, sticky liquid had made a real difference until soon I was applying it every day. Mum noticed but didn't mind – she knew I was growing up and wanted to experiment with my appearance. But the more I applied, the more I needed. It was as if in Hayley's world, nothing would ever be good enough.

Soon, I'd reached the end of primary school. On one of my last days there, a girl called Kayleigh approached me at the school gate, threw me up against it, and pinned me there. I was simply terrified. Mum was waiting to pick me up and saw everything. It was home time and lots of children were spilling out of school so the playground was packed. Above it all I heard a lone voice – it belonged to Kayleigh's older sister.

'Go on Kayleigh, hit her,' she shouted.

I was utterly petrified. The attack had been completely unprovoked and I didn't know what to do or even how to defend myself. A voice taunted me inside my head.

*I'm ugly, that's why she wants to hit me!*

Despite all the pretty clothes Mum bought me, despite the mascara, despite everything, I felt totally worthless. Maybe I deserved it because I never, ever felt as pretty as the other girls. Kayleigh knew it, that's why she'd singled me out from the others. But Mum had seen and now she was furious. She marched straight up to Kayleigh and gave her a mouthful. Mum was just sticking up for me but I was mortified because everyone was looking over at us. It was my worst nightmare – I felt as exposed as if I'd been standing there stark naked.

'Don't you ever lay your hands on my daughter again, do you understand?' Mum was saying, her voice carried loud across the playground.

Kayleigh nodded meekly but Mum still wasn't happy so she went to see the headmaster. I felt awkward standing there as she recounted everything she'd just witnessed. The head promised to take action but after that day, I was afraid. The thought of Kayleigh's sister waiting for me at secondary school in September made my stomach twist with anxiety. Throughout the summer holidays I worried about it until it plagued me. I imagined walking through the gate of my new school only to be stopped in my tracks by the two sisters. The resulting 'fight scene' played over and over inside my head until it became so real that I could almost touch it. I imagined myself splattered with my own blood – the thought of it made my heart race. The only way I could calm myself was to move more furniture or tidy my bedroom. Soon, even that wasn't enough, so I'd sit down and apply even more mascara. All three things helped me feel better, the rituals acting like a soothing balm on my fraught mind.

By the time I started secondary school I was so obsessed with mascara that now I wouldn't be seen dead without it. I needed it just to feel normal. Instead of worrying about the fishpond or moving furniture, I turned in on myself.

*What else could I do to change my appearance?* I wondered.

I searched inside Mum's vanity box and found more stuff to help conceal the real me. The real Hayley was still there but now she was buried underneath layers and layers of makeup.

It became my mask and helped hide the insecure and terrified little girl I'd become. Only, the more makeup I wore, the more others judged me. I was labelled vain – a Barbie doll – but the cruel reality was that I was just a frightened little girl, too scared to reveal who she really was to the rest of the world. I could hide behind my makeup. After that, every spare moment I had, I'd stand in front of the mirror in the girls' toilets at school and apply yet another layer. Slowly, I built up my armour but instead of using mascara, I dabbed on foundation too. It made my face look washed out, like a blank canvas, so I painted on my cheeks and filled in my mouth. I used blusher to give me back some colour and a little lip-gloss to accentuate my lips and balance my face out. I loved the way the makeup made me feel. I looked more feminine but more importantly, I felt accepted. Deep down, I knew I'd never be beautiful enough because I set myself impossibly high standards but the makeup gave me enough confidence to feel as though I was good enough to belong. I started hanging around with the popular girls. Unlike me, they didn't wear makeup. Most of my friends were black and naturally pretty so they didn't need it. I never considered myself as good as them and no matter how much makeup I applied, I'd knew I'd never feel as attractive. The makeup just took the edge off my low self-esteem. I convinced myself mascara and lip-gloss would make everything okay again but the reality was nothing ever would because I never quite came up to scratch.

Mum noticed and started to nag me to take it off. It wasn't the fact I wore it which annoyed her, just how much I used. Some mornings, she'd be at the bottom of the stairs waiting to 'check' my face before I left for school.

'Take some of that off – you've got far too much on!'

I was a typical teenager and now I'd started secondary school, I had attitude to go with it.

'What's too much make up?' I replied cockily. 'Anyway, you can't wear enough...'

But Mum was furious.

'Now you listen to me young lady, you need to take some of that makeup off and you need to take it off now.'

My heart thudded with panic. I couldn't take it off because if I did then everyone would see how ugly I was. Instead, I made a big show of checking my watch. I'd spent ages applying and reapplying my makeup that morning. It was as near perfect as it'd ever be and I wasn't going to take it off for Mum or anyone else. I glanced up at Lauren who was waiting by the front door.

'If I take it off now I'll be late – we'll both be late,' I said gesturing over towards my big sister. 'But I will take it off, promise. I'll take it off on my way to school.'

Mum shook her head with despair. She knew she didn't have time to argue because she couldn't be late for work.

'Okay, okay, but you better do it, otherwise I won't be happy.'

I nodded, opened up the door and pulled it shut.

'So, are you going it take it off then?' Lauren asked as we turned the corner of the street.

'Nah, course not. I just said that to keep her happy.' I smiled and linked my arm through my sister's and we ran to make up for lost time.

I didn't remove my makeup because without it, I couldn't function. It became my comfort blanket and life-support wrapped into one. The more people nagged me to take it off, the more I dug my heels in. Everyone labelled me a rebel but my new-found attitude stemmed from fear, not arrogance. The thought of washing off my foundation and eye makeup made me feel physically sick. I didn't realise it then, but I was slowly becoming obsessive and it was spiralling out of control.

Occasionally, I'd spot Kayleigh standing in the school corridor but by now she avoided all eye contact with me because I was one of the popular girls. As long as I kept in with the group then everything would be fine. I tried my best to emulate them and kept my hair as perfect as possible. Nanny Linda ironed my clothes every day. She loved to iron so it wasn't a chore for her. I was grateful because now I couldn't stand dirty marks or creases in my clothes. I changed my uniform all the time and, if I spilt food or even splashed a drop of juice, I'd take off my jumper. It didn't matter if it was freezing cold because I couldn't bear to look dirty or scruffy. I was just as obsessive when it came to the length of my school skirt. It had to be just so: enough above my knee so that it didn't look prissy, but not too short because I didn't want to look like a slag. Whenever I passed Kayleigh with my new found friends I couldn't help but feel a little smug.

*Not so big now, are we?*

Not long afterwards, one of the older girls got into a fight with Kayleigh's sister. I was elated because she'd finally got her comeuppance after egging her little sister on to smack me. All those times I'd worried about being beaten up and now there she was – a crumpled mess on the floor.

As my obsession with makeup worsened, so did my fear of eating in public. It'd always been there but, unlike the fishpond, it was one fear which never went away.

One morning, during my first summer holiday from secondary school, Mum decided to take me and my two sisters shopping for new uniforms. Zara had had a growth spurt and needed some new trousers. Lauren and I also needed kitting out. Hipster trousers were really trendy at the time and the tighter, the better. But the shops near us didn't sell trousers like that.

'We could go shopping in Croydon instead?' Mum suggested.

Zara and Lauren were beyond excitement. Croydon was a much bigger place with loads of shops but I didn't say a word. The thought of going petrified me because Croydon was a place where all the big gangs hung out.

'Do we have to go?' I asked anxiously.

Mum was adamant.

'Yes, Hayley, we do.'

Try as I might I couldn't shake the new vision out of my head – one where a gang was attacking Mum and terrorising me and my sisters in the middle of the street. Later that day, Mum drove and, although the traffic was heavy, it didn't take us long to reach Croydon. She parked up and we started to shop, making our way along the high street. For the next few hours we wandered around but all the time I was constantly alert, watching and waiting for someone to attack us. I couldn't relax and enjoy myself because inside I felt so anxious. I prayed the day would end.

'You're quiet, Hayley.' Mum remarked as we walked along.

It was true; I'd hardly said a word because I was too busy worrying.

'I'll tell you what,' she said suddenly, 'Let's go to McDonalds.'

Lauren whooped with delight and so did Zara because having lunch at McDonalds was a huge treat. I longed to feel as excited only I couldn't because I knew McDonald's was where teenagers hung out and I was terrified there'd be gangs waiting for us.

*This is it, this is where the attack will happen*, the voice warned.

As soon as we pushed the door open my stomach clenched. It was Saturday and the place was heaving with hordes of teenagers. My throat constricted and seemed to close – I felt intimidated just being there. Although I followed the others inside my immediate thought was *I'm not eating in here*.

'What are you all having then?' Mum asked.

My heart was banging as if it was too big inside my chest and the palms of my hands felt clammy. The last thing I wanted to do was eat. I couldn't eat because of the teenagers, but also because I'd have to eat in front of strangers. I'd just walked into my worst nightmare. Lauren and Zara were hungry and ordered a burger and fries quickly, and then it was my turn. Mum turned to face me, she was waiting. My eyes nervously darted around looking at them all sitting on plastic chairs, perched against bright plastic tables. It was really busy, crammed with people talking and eating. My stomach turned.

*It was too busy.*

'Err, I'm not hungry,' I said casting my eyes downwards so that Mum wouldn't see me lying.

'Come on, Hayley, you haven't eaten for hours; you must want something?'

Lauren turned to look and I felt my face flush. I was hot and embarrassed, trapped inside McDonald's, with too many people and too many pairs of eyes watching me. Mum didn't understand and refused to take no for an answer. I started to panic because the long queue had dispersed quickly and now we were next in line.

'Can I help?' A smiley girl behind the till called, beckoning us forward.

My heart was thumping so loud that I wondered if anyone else could hear it.

*Why did I feel so scared?*

Mum placed the order and turned to me, along with Lauren and Zara. Even the girl behind the till looked at me. They were all standing there, waiting for me to decide. I felt under pressure. The palms of my hands were wet as though they were slowly melting.

'Hayley?' Mum asked.

I had to pick something, anything to stop them from looking at me. Images of food on the illuminated sign above the till whirred and blurred before my eyes – there was too much to choose from. Someone tutted loudly behind – I had to make a decision and I had to make one quickly.

'I'll have the chicken,' I blurted out.

It was the first thing to come into my head. I heard a collective sigh of relief from my family and even the girl behind the till as she bleeped in the final part of the order. Mum told us to go and find somewhere to sit. My eyes scanned the room; I need a table – one where I could eat without facing strangers, but Lauren had other ideas. She ran over and plonked herself down in an empty seat right next to the window and Zara followed.

'Here?' I asked, slightly appalled.

Lauren and Zara looked up at me.

'Yeah, here,' Lauren huffed.

'Err, there must be somewhere else,' I said, looking around.

Only there wasn't because nowhere else was free. I was stuck – in full view of the window and everyone inside the restaurant. I flopped down into the seat opposite and felt utterly miserable as I glanced out of the window. A passing gang of teenage boys caught my gaze and stared back at me. My stomach cramped because it felt like a living hell.

'I think we should move,' I said, suddenly getting up.

Lauren refused to budge.

'I'm not moving,' she said, folding her arms.

I was just about to argue when Mum slid the red plastic tray onto the table in front of us.

'There you go,' she said breezily. 'I bet you're all starving.'

But I wasn't hungry, I felt sick to my stomach. As the others tucked into their food I stared hopelessly out of the window. I was surrounded by my family but I'd never felt so alone. I just wanted to be normal; to be able to rip open the bag and eat my food like everyone else, only I couldn't because something was stopping me. I couldn't see it or touch it but it was as real as the people sitting next to me. It was a fear of being judged and talked about, a fear of eating the food in front of me. I grabbed the top of the brown paper bag and scrunched it down with my fingers.

'Aren't you hungry?' Mum asked.

'Not really. Would it be okay if I took it home and warmed it up for later?'

Mum sighed and put her burger down on the greaseproof wrapper. It took all the strength I had to smile but I needed to reassure her. I didn't want her worrying because I did enough of that for everyone. I couldn't tell her the real reason that I was too scared to eat in front of people. At home I knew everything would be okay because back home, everything was familiar and safe.

'Okay,' Mum finally agreed. 'I'll warm it up in the microwave.'

I carried the little brown bag around in my hand for the rest of the afternoon. Hunger pangs gripped me as the hours passed but still I refused to eat or even take a nibble. The chicken and chips were stone cold and looked a little congealed by the time we'd reached home but I didn't care. I placed my food on a plate inside the microwave and watched as the light blinked on and the meal turned around and around.

'Careful,' Mum said taking it out and putting it down on the table in front of me. 'It's really hot. Don't burn yourself!'

The chicken didn't taste as good as I knew it would've back in the restaurant but at least I could eat it without worrying.

On our next visit to McDonalds I brought my food home again to warm up inside the microwave. But this time, I only took a bite before I had to run straight to toilet where I was sick. I felt wretched because I thought I'd finally found a way to beat the fear, only I hadn't. Instead, like the food inside the bag, it'd just packed itself up and followed me home.

COMING CLEAN
LIVING WITH OCD

**CHAPTER 5**

# *BEING BULLIED, MOVING HOME AND LOSING MY WAY*

MUM'S RELATIONSHIP WITH Paul went from strength to strength and soon it became so serious that he moved in with us for good. It seemed as though everyone else was moving on with their lives, everyone apart from me. My compulsions and fears pinned me down and held me back in every area of my life. By now my makeup had all but taken over until soon, I'd even given up moving bedroom furniture around.

After the summer, I moved up into Year 8. While the confidence which went with not being in the lowest year helped, I was far from cured. Underneath my makeup I was still as insecure as I'd ever been. In fact, if I got a speck of mud on my shoes, I'd go straight to the toilet so I could wipe it off. I became obsessed with being as clean as possible and I'd wash my hands constantly in the sink at school.

One afternoon, I returned home to find Mum really shaken up. She'd been in a car accident but weirdly it hadn't been that which had upset her, it'd been the children from a nearby school who'd crowded in the playground and laughed as she'd climbed out of her car battered and bruised.

'You should have seen them, Paul,' she said, clearly still shaken up. 'They were just laughing at me. They were kids as well. This place is getting worse, it's getting rougher.'

Mum's words must have been an omen because sure enough, just a few months later, I was walking past a local boys' school in London, when one of the lads took off his belt and beat me with it for no reason.

'I didn't even touch him or go near him. He just did it – he just attacked me,' I wept to Mum.

She raised her eyes and looked over at Paul as if to say *'See what I mean? I can't bring my girls up around here.'*

The rest of the school year dragged by in an endless cycle of hand-washing and makeup until soon the holidays had almost arrived. With summer fast approaching, I decided to have some copper highlights put in my long dark brown hair. Mum had taken me to a salon at Clapham Junction and paid for me to have them done. As I left the hairdressers I felt different, I even felt good about myself because I knew my hair looked really nice. Only one person wasn't quite as impressed and her name was Amber. Amber was a pretty, mixed-race girl who had previously been good friends with a pal of mine called Ceyonne. However, the two drifted apart so Ceyonne and I became pals, much to Amber's annoyance. She'd had her nose put out of joint and, for some reason, she didn't approve of a white girl like me taking her place. So, as soon as she saw my new hairstyle she used it to have a go at me.

'Hey, what's with you?' Amber shouted one afternoon staring over towards me.

'What?' I said turning around with a start.

Amber was standing directly behind me. I turned and she was so close that I could feel her breath on my face.

'What's with all this?' She said tugging at a clump of my hair.

I was confused; I didn't have a clue what she was talking about.

'My hair?' I guessed correctly.

She nodded and folded her arms as if waiting for an explanation.

'I've just had it done.'

But it was clear that Amber was furious.

'Yeah, look, with copper highlights,' she said, dipping her own head down, pointing towards the back of it. 'Copper highlights just like mine, innit. What's wrong with you?' she said, giving me a shove. 'Are you jealous? Are you jealous of me and that why you want to look like me?'

I shook my head, my hair looked nothing like hers but still she wouldn't stop.

'Is that why you want to copy me, because you're a stupid little white girl.'

I blinked back my horror. I hadn't even noticed that Amber had copper highlights because her hair was so much darker than mine. But now she was accusing me of copying her.

'No, no,' I tried to explain. 'It's my mum, she made me an appointment and...'

But she refused to listen and balled her fists as though she was about to smack me.

'You're sad, you know that?' she said, leaning in.

She looked down and sneered as I steeled myself, waiting for her punch. Only it didn't happen. She turned to walk away but as she did, she stopped and turned back towards me. 'From now on you wanna watch yourself...'

Her threat left me quaking with fear. Amber wasn't someone you messed with but I hadn't intended to upset her. After that day, she used every opportunity to target me. Once she kicked me. Then, the following day she tripped me up and I landed in a crumpled heap on the floor.

'Ooops!' she cackled.

She even started on Ceyonne.

'Why do you want to be friends with a little white girl, eh?' she asked.

It was racism, pure and simple, only Amber was mixed race and I was white. I was the victim but as a pupil in a multi-cultural London school, I found it impossible to complain or speak out. I knew if I did, then Amber would target me twice as much.

To make matters worse, Lauren, who was in the year above me, was slim and pretty with long blonde hair, so she suffered twice as much. In particular, there was one black girl who targeted Lauren for her looks and even threw bricks at her. In a bid to protect ourselves, we'd try and walk home together. One afternoon, I missed Lauren and was walking with my friend Rachel past Clapham Common when Amber caught up with us. Just her being there unnerved me but then she did something which took my breath away – she linked her arm in mine. My senses went into full alert but Amber explained she just wanted to be friends.

'You and me, we're good,' she insisted.

There was another girl with her who I didn't recognise. She was much older than us. As we walked along it became apparent it was Amber's sister and she was even scarier! Rachel was still with us because she didn't want to leave me alone with them. But the more she refused to go, the more threatening Amber's sister became.

'Tell your mate to go otherwise she's going to get stabbed,' she warned.

I gulped because I believed every single word. I was so frightened that I begged Rachel to leave. I didn't want to be left alone with them but I didn't want her to get hurt because of me. She was reluctant but I insisted.

'Okay, but I'll see you tomorrow,' she said.

As she left, I noticed Amber and her sister smirk at one another. My stomach twisted inside. Suddenly Amber changed direction and insisted we take a short cut across the common. I was scared because it was totally deserted and I didn't want to be with them.

'We're going to be friends from now on', she said, patting me on the hand.

Only I didn't believe her. Once we'd reached a clearing, Amber unlatched her arm and pushed me away so hard that I fell onto the ground. I winced as she and her sister took it in turns to kick me. I lifted my hands up to protect my face but they kicked me in the chest and stomach instead. The pain was excruciating.

'If it's my hair, I'll promise I'll change it!' I pleaded with them.

I was terrified that her sister would produce a knife at any moment and stab me. Amber's face contorted with fury as she continued to kick me. I was crying my heart out; my cheeks were streaked black with mascara. I believed they'd kill me there and then but, just when I thought I couldn't take anymore, they stopped. My eyes were all swollen from crying but I looked up at Amber who was standing over me. She signalled to her sister and together they pulled me back up to my feet. I flinched, waiting for something else, but there was nothing. Amber cleared her throat and spoke.

'Right, you've had your beating. Just don't tell anyone what we've done to you or we'll come after you, understand?'

She looked over at her sister who nodded in agreement.

'We're friends now. We're good, okay?'

I agreed, grateful I'd escaped alive.

'And remember; don't tell anyone, not a soul.'

'I won't,' I promised. My whole body was trembling but I was relieved that it was over.

'Now, where do you live?' Amber asked.

Her question jolted me because I didn't want her to know. My mind raced as I tried to think of an answer. I couldn't tell her the truth but I didn't want to lie either, because God only knows what she'd do then. Instead, I named a busy street just around the corner from mine. It was on a main route with lots of houses on it so I knew she'd never know.

'Okay. Do you want us to walk you home?'

I refused but Amber insisted. The long walk home was excruciating because I half expected them to start on me again, but they didn't. As we turned into the busy street I insisted I'd be fine.

'It's just down there,' I said pointing off towards mid distance. 'Thanks for walking me back.'

'Okay, but we'll wait here to make sure you get home okay,' Amber replied.

My heart sank to my knees. I continued to walk along the street wondering what on earth I could do. As I neared the corner of my street I glanced back but they were still there. I lifted my hand to wave but they didn't budge. I gulped, turned, and headed straight into the garden of a house on the corner. I pretended to walk up to the front door. Thankfully, the house had a recessed porch so I hid inside it, tucking myself tightly against the door, praying that no one would open it. I waited a few more moments before popping my head out to look towards the end of the street. They'd gone! I was battered, bruised and utterly terrified. Hitching up my school bag up on my shoulder, I ran as fast as I could around the corner and into my street. I didn't stop running until I'd reached my backdoor. Once there, I broke down and told Mum and Nanny Linda everything. Mum was furious. She rang the school and demanded to speak to the headmaster. He told her to come in so he could talk to her in person.

'I want something done,' she told him, 'You should see the state of my daughter.'

I'd never seen her so angry.

It took a few hours but, eventually, I calmed down. The following morning, I dreaded going into school because I was terrified I'd bump into Amber.

'She wouldn't dare touch you', Mum insisted – but I didn't believe her.

Thankfully, I didn't see Amber but I did see Rachel.

'What happened, after I left?' she asked as soon as she saw me.

I started to shake.

'I felt so bad, leaving you. I didn't want to go. I've been up all night worried sick. I thought they'd stab you or something!'

Rachel was garbling but I didn't want to tell her. Besides, Amber had made me promise not to breathe a word. But Mum knew and so did the head. I needed to talk to someone so I told her everything. Her eyes widened with shock.

'But you mustn't say anything.' I said, grabbing her arm. 'Amber mustn't know I've told you otherwise she'll come looking for me.'

Rachel promised and I believed her so I still don't know how Amber found out. Days later, I was told she was looking for me. Sure enough, Mum went to see the head who explained in no uncertain terms that Amber's family weren't the sort of people you 'messed with'.

'We've got to tread carefully because she comes from a very violent family', he explained.

'So, in other words you're not going to do anything?'

The headmaster leaned back in his chair, looked at Mum and then at me.

'My hands are tied, I'm afraid.'

Mum was so angry that she immediately pulled both Lauren and me out of school even though the summer holidays were only weeks away. By now, Mum was sick of London, with its crime and anti-social behaviour. Within weeks, she and Paul decided to up sticks, sell the house and move us all to Dormansland near Lingfield on the Surrey/ West Sussex border.

'It'll be a fresh start for us all,' she told us.

And it was, in more ways than one because, shortly afterwards, Paul and Mum announced that they were getting married.

'I'm not calling him Dad,' I whispered to Lauren.

I meant it. Paul wasn't my dad. I only had one Dad and he lived miles away in London.

After the move, I missed my dad so much that he'd climb in his car and drive down to Sussex, just to see us. He wouldn't come in the house but park up outside in the street. Lauren, Zara and I would run to him as soon as we saw his car pull up and we'd sit inside it chatting and laughing. When the hour was up, we'd go back inside and Dad would drive all the way home again. It was a strange arrangement but I never asked Mum why Dad didn't ever come in, I just accepted it because it was better than not seeing him at all.

Mum and Paul married in a low-key affair at a local register office. Mum didn't wear white; she didn't even have any bridesmaids. I was disappointed that we wouldn't get the chance to be bridesmaids but Nanny Linda explained it was because Mum didn't want any fuss. She said that when Mum and Dad had got married it'd been a huge affair.

'It was one of the flashiest weddings I've ever been to,' she told me. 'Your mum looked so stunning that she ended up on the front cover of a bridal magazine.'

I knew it was true because I'd seen the picture. Mum had always been pretty but never more so than on her wedding day to Dad. Maybe it was because she'd had such a big wedding the first time round that she didn't want the same again. On the actual day, instead of a bridal gown, she wore a tight-fitting black designer suit. Afterwards, at the reception she changed into a lovely long silk evening dress. Mum looked beautiful, everyone said so. She looked so lovely that I felt proud to be her daughter. Afterwards, she and Paul flew away on honeymoon while Nanny Linda looked after us. Meanwhile, we started at our new school. I was so desperate to fit in that I tried my very best to look 'perfect' every hour of every day. Of course, there's no such thing as perfect, but as long as I performed my daily rituals and looked my best, then I felt safe. I was terrified of a repeat of what had happened at my last school with Amber. Thankfully, Lauren and I were not only accepted, we were held up to be something 'special'. We were the two new 'cool' girls from London, and I was determined to live up to the role, anything to stop the real, insecure Hayley from seeping out. Every morning, I'd flick on the bedroom light and spend hours applying my makeup for school. With my standards higher than ever, I'd often apply it but if I felt it didn't look right or I wasn't happy, I'd take out cotton wool and cleanser, wipe it off and start all over again. Some days I'd apply so much foundation that it'd become patchy so I'd sit and re-do it again. There was no end to it. Often, Lauren would be standing, waiting by the door. She didn't understand why I needed to look the way I did but then, she wasn't like me. Lauren was slim, blonde and gorgeous and I felt dull, standing in her shadow, so I applied more makeup. The ritual was relentless. No one had called me ugly; it was just how I felt inside. My obsession often made Lauren late for school and sometimes she'd leave without me. But even when I was at school I couldn't escape my compulsion. During break I wouldn't hang out with other girls, instead I'd apply more makeup and then wash my hands for fear of germs. The only time I avoided washing was when it came to PE. The hot steam mixed with the smell of other people's body odour in the school showers made me feel nauseous. PE was a particular torture for me because there was always a real chance I'd get 'dirty'. I didn't want to wash with everyone else because I knew I'd never be clean enough. I hated the school showers as my obsession with germs and dirt grew. I convinced myself I'd come out of the showers even dirtier than I went in because other people's germs would be there mixed in the water swirling by my feet. Instead, I used every excuse in the book. The gym teacher must have thought I was on a permanent period because I gave the same excuse so many times. One afternoon, I even lied and told her I had a verruca on my foot when all the time I was terrified in case I caught one from the filthy floor of the communal changing rooms. I was certain I'd catch a disease just from walking across the room. Every time I escaped the showers the more I thought about dirt and germs.

My new school uniform was dire – a pale blue shirt coupled with an itchy navy jumper and black hipster trousers. In many ways, despite my compulsions, I was still a typical teenager with an attitude. I disliked my new school and I hated one teacher in particular. She singled me out from the start because it was clear she disapproved of all the makeup I wore. On a few occasions she dragged me unceremoniously out of class and into the toilet where she demanded that I wash it off. I refused and was given detention but I didn't care because it just gave me more time to apply my makeup. The teacher and some of the pupils thought I was vain, but I wasn't. My makeup was a compulsion – just like jumping the fishpond, moving furniture, and even my fear of food. I couldn't explain to them but I had to perform each and every one so I could function. I was only 14, and I didn't realise I was ill; neither did anyone else because I hid it well. Instead my illness came across as 'attitude' and my teachers simply gave up on me. In many ways, I was a complete nightmare. I missed my Dad and hated Paul telling me what to do. I didn't want to admit it but I was jealous – jealous because, in my mind, Mum had chosen Paul over us.

As the months passed so my behaviour became worse until one day, Mum told us she was pregnant. Instantly it changed everything because I was excited about getting a new brother or sister. Somehow I hoped this new baby would help bond us together. When my half-sister Jasmine was born, I was absolutely thrilled because we had a new baby to fuss over. Me and my sisters fawned over Jasmine and, instead of just one mum, she had five – us, Mum and Nanny Linda. Despite my best hopes, my relationship with my stepdad Paul became unbearable. Paul was house-proud and liked things to be just so. In many ways, he was just like me, only it wound me up. Maybe there wasn't room in one house for two perfectionists, who knows? One of Paul's rules was that we remove our shoes whenever we entered the house to stop the carpet getting filthy. One day, he asked me to take off my shoes but I refused.

'I said take your shoes off Hayley, now!'

But instead of doing as I was told I rested my hands on my hips and pulled a face.

'No!'

'I said, take your shoes off, and take them off now!'

But I didn't want Paul telling me what I could and couldn't do.

'No, you can't boss me around – you're not my dad.'

I knew I was being a total bitch but I couldn't help it. I missed Dad and having this new man in our house felt wrong. The more I answered him back, the more it enraged him until soon poor Mum had reached her wits end. Unlike me, my sisters obeyed. Lauren didn't like confrontation, and Zara was young so she tended to do as she was told.

One day, I was lounging around in the house when Paul came to look for me.

'You need to hoover up,' he said, trying to assert his authority.

But I was having none of it.

'No,' I huffed before turning back to look at the page of the magazine I was reading.

Paul saw red and started to argue so I shouted back at him. 'You wanker!'

The words came spilling out of my mouth before I'd even had a chance to think what I was saying. Paul was boiling with rage. I realised I'd pushed him too far and I jumped to my feet and ran straight upstairs to my bedroom. The house was modern but had been fitted with Victorian-style wooden doors. My bedroom door had a large metal key in the lock so I turned it and locked myself in. Paul was ranting and raving outside and I could hear Mum trying to calm him down.

'Either she goes or I do,' he shouted.

I wanted Mum to be angry with him but she wasn't.

'And I want her gone by the time I get back,' he was saying.

I heard footsteps on the stairs – Paul's footsteps – as he slammed the front door shut. Suddenly the house was quiet and still and I wondered what Mum would do. I was sitting there waiting to come out of my bedroom when I saw her hand push a black bin liner underneath the door.

'Pack up your things. You go. You leave now,' Mum said simply.

Tears pricked at the back of my eyes because I knew I'd pushed her too far. I thought of Nanny Linda, but she was miles away staying with Uncle Duncan and his wife up north.

*She'd never allow this to happen. Nanny Linda would rather take a knife to her stomach than let me leave this house in the dead of night.* I thought bitterly.

I glanced at the clock on the side. It was 9pm. Surely Mum was just angry.

*She didn't really want me to leave, did she?*

But her silence said it all. I was so angry that by now I *wanted* to leave. My teenage ego wouldn't allow me to stay. I crammed as many things as I could fit into the bin liner and looked around for my mobile phone. I cursed when I realised it had no credit on it, it was useless. I didn't have any money or clue where I'd go – I didn't care. I wasn't wanted so I'd leave – it was as simple as that. As I closed the front door, I expected Mum to come running after me, only she didn't. My pride refused to let me turn back so I headed along the street and through Dormansland wood in the pitch dark. I was absolutely terrified but, with nowhere to go, I headed for the lights of the train station. The only house I knew how to get to was my Auntie Julie's. She lived right next to Streatham Common station so I knew I could reach her safely. I looked at the train times – there was no through train – I'd have to change at East Croydon. I didn't have a penny on me so I watched out for the guard as I bunked the ride with no ticket. By the time I reached Auntie Julie's house I was spent, both emotionally and physically. Auntie Julie is Dad's sister so, naturally, she called my father to let him know I was safe. They decided I could stay there for the next few weeks until the dust had settled. Julie was a single parent with a young son to look after so she was glad of the extra pair of hands. Soon I was doing the childcare as well as helping out with the shopping and laundry. I didn't mind because I couldn't face home or school and I didn't miss either. My behaviour had simply gone off the rails. Sure enough, Julie found it difficult living with a sulking 14-year-old, so it was decided that I'd go to live with Dad. Meanwhile, everyone wanted to get involved. Granddad Bert wanted to call social services even though Dad had taken me in. Although I knew he wanted me, the talk of social services made me feel as though I was a burden to everyone. By this time, Dad and Carol were running a busy pub in Tunbridge Wells, so I stayed in the flat upstairs. However, my new way of life didn't seem quite as exciting as I'd first thought when, a few weeks later, a huge fight broke out in the pub. Dad tried to sort it out but it was so rowdy that I was soon on the phone to Mum begging to come home.

'I hate it here, please can I come back?' I pleaded, as I sobbed down the phone.

The noise of the fight downstairs had shocked me. I was still only a girl and now I needed to go home. For all my teenage bravado, I realised that I actually had quite a nice life in Dormansland, and that the grass wasn't greener on the other side. Mum listened and passed the phone over to Paul, saying I owed him an apology.

'I'm sorry,' I wept. 'Please can I come home?'

There was a silence on the other end of the line and, at first, I thought he'd say no, but Paul was better than that.

'Okay. Do you want me to come and get you?'

I could have cried with relief. It wasn't that I didn't love my Dad – I loved him with all my heart – it was just I wasn't nearly as tough or brave as I thought. In the end, I missed over a month of school and, by the time I returned, I was 15 years old. It was towards the end of the summer term and some of the kids from school had been sent to paint over graffiti in the centre of town. As soon as I spotted my old friends my heart lifted.

'Can I help?' I asked reaching for a paintbrush so I could get stuck in.

But I gasped with shock when they refused and some even turned away. I guessed their parents must've heard about my great escape and told them to steer well clear of me: the naughty girl from London. I was shocked just how much I'd missed school but now I was back it was clear everything had changed. No one wanted to talk to me or even know me now. Stupidly, I thought it was going to be normal, that I could just pick up where I'd left off but I realised life isn't like that. With only weeks to go, I decided I may as well not be there at all so I bunked off. The following day, when the usual teacher stopped me in the corridor and told me to remove my makeup, instead of doing as I was told, I calmly picked up my bag and walked out of the building. I spent the rest of the afternoon on a park bench, lonely and left out. But no one thought to ask me why I'd refused or why I acted the way I did. They presumed I was out of control and, in many ways, I was.

One Saturday night I was watching *Stars in their Eyes* on TV with Nanny Linda when a bunch of backing dancers came on behind the main tribute act. I was simply mesmerised. Nanny Linda saw and turned to me.

'I reckon you could do that, Hayley', she said, pointing at the TV screen.

'Me?' I replied. I loved to dance but I was hardly a professional.

'Why not? And not just dance. I reckon you'd be great at presenting a programme or something. You'd make a brilliant TV host because you've got such a lovely personality.'

I looked at Nanny and back at the TV screen.

*Could I do that?* I wondered.

Despite the fact people would be watching, strangely, something about it really tempted me. Maybe it'd be a sure-fire way to be loved and accepted, I didn't know but, after that moment, the thought of a career in TV appealed to me even though I didn't have a clue how to get into it.

In my final school year, and in a bid to win back my friends, I became the class clown. I was so desperate not to get picked on or bullied by the other kids that I regularly told my teachers to fuck off. My mates loved it and I soon got a reputation. I had no respect for authority; instead I bunked off school and burned things on the Bunsen burner in science class to get attention. I decided to live up to my new and disruptive title. My old friends soon came swarming back. It gave me confidence to play up to the teachers even more but really it was just a cry for help. Deep down, I wanted someone to ask why I bunked off and why I ran off to sit on a park bench instead of removing my makeup. In fact, I wanted them to ask me why I needed to wear so much makeup yet, despite it all, despite my appalling behaviour, no one ever did.

One day, I was sent to the head of year's office for talking in class.

'Why do you behave like this, Hayley?' he asked, 'What is your problem exactly?'

I thought for a moment. I knew I could make up a load of old bull or I could just be honest and tell the truth, so I did.

'When I was in London, I was badly bullied. I don't want it to happen again so that's why I am like I am. I am never, ever going to be pushed around like that again.'

I needed to explain why I acted the way I did. I wanted him to understand that my disruptive behaviour stemmed through a fear of being bullied and rejected. But instead of trying to understand, the teacher laughed. It made me feel less than worthless.

'For goodness sake, stop making excuses and stop telling lies! Now pick up your bag and go to the isolation unit. It'll give you some time to reflect on your behaviour both in class and in school.'

The teacher's reaction made me feel like sticking up two fingers to the rest of the world. If he didn't believe me, then who would? I sat in isolation that day but, instead of general reflection, I stared at *my* reflection and daubed on even more makeup. The teachers ordered me to take it off but when I told them I couldn't, no one asked *why not*? No one thought to look deeper or scratch below the surface to ask just why I seemed so troubled and disruptive. They labelled me a rebel so I acted like one. I convinced myself I had no real friends, so what did it matter? So, when a friend asked if I wanted a drag of her cigarette, I did, not because I wanted to, but because I wanted to fit in. It was peer pressure, pure and simple. I didn't like the smell of cigarette smoke or the way it seeped into my clothes or the skin on my fingers. But I smoked when I was with them because, when I smoked, it suppressed my appetite and I became thinner and more attractive. However, my new habit also meant I washed and scrubbed my hands constantly. My compulsions slowly blurred into a vicious cycle of hand washing, smoking and makeup as I counted down my last days at school. Looking back, I wish I'd have worked harder and stopped trying so hard to make other people like me. I wish I'd have felt confident enough in myself and my abilities. Now I was popular but for all the wrong reasons. I was liked but I was also running scared. For the first time in my life, I didn't really care about my grades or learning – I had no motivation or real desire to do well so, when I flunked my GSCEs, it was no great surprise. I didn't even have a back-up plan. I didn't realise it then but my ritualistic behaviour was slowly taking over until it had all but consumed me.

## CHAPTER 6

# *WORKING WOMAN*

WITH VERY FEW decent grades from my exams to back me up, I decided to go into hairdressing. There was no great strategy behind it, I just knew the position would allow me time to adjust my makeup, do my hair and wash my hands without being detected.

I was recommended for an interview at a small hairdressing salon through the career advisor at school. The boss there was lovely. She was an attractive middle-aged woman who not only owned the salon but ran it too. When she told me I'd got the job I was so thrilled that I almost punched the air. At last, I'd got something through my own merit but the job sounded much more glamorous than it was. My apprentice position generally meant someone who could sweep, dust, and wash customers' hair. Although the work was monotonous, in many ways I was in my element, because it gave me an excuse to spend the day tidying up. The only part of the job I detested was washing the greasy and lank hair of strangers. With this to contend with, my fear of catching germs intensified, sending my ritual hand washing up to another level. Soon, I was standing at the basins scrubbing my hands up to 60 times a day.

I'd only been working at the salon a week when an old lady walked in through the door. She wanted a set and blow dry but her hair needed to be washed first. The salon was based in a side road so it relied on regular customers, particularly older clients who had more time on their hands. I took the lady's coat and was asked to wash her hair. I started to run water into the basin but it was too hot so I waited a moment longer until it'd run a little cooler. When it'd finally reached the correct temperature I soaked the old lady's hair through and absentmindedly squeezed a dollop of shampoo into my hand. The water instantly thinned her hair, sticking it to her scalp and that's when I saw it, a huge bulbous mole on top of her head. My heart banged inside my chest as I tried to calm myself down. She was clean, unlike some of the other customers, but the mole was huge and looked as if it'd been cast from a lump of skin-coloured jelly. I shuddered as I frothed the shampoo into a lather and tried my best to wash around it.

*I can't do this,* the voice screamed inside my head.

But I forced myself to carry on because I had to do it. As my hands carefully worked around it I tried to imagine the little old lady was Nanny Rose or Nanny Linda. I manoeuvred my fingers upwards but it looked so ripe and ready to pop that I was terrified one of my fingernails would catch and burst it. The more I tried not to think about it, the more I focused on it. It sounds shallow but I felt ill because I was convinced if the mole popped, then I'd be covered in the old lady's blood and germs. I couldn't even look away because if I did then I was sure to catch it with a sharp fingernail. Suddenly and without warning, the little old lady shifted in her chair. Her head flicked to the side and that's when it happened, my nail caught the mole. I felt her wince beneath me as I tried to remember how to breathe. The shampoo had frothed up and it was now covering her scalp – I couldn't see a thing – I was washing blind! Suddenly, the mole snagged against my nail only this time, it was me who flinched. The woman asked me what was wrong but I daren't say. The manageress was standing there, watching me and I didn't want to balls up my one and only job opportunity. However, the fear of germs set my senses on high alert and it took all the strength I had just to rinse her hair off. All I wanted to do was run to the toilet and be sick but somehow I held my nerve and showed her back to the stylist's chair.

'Everything alright, Hayley?' the manageress whispered as I brushed past.

'Yes,' I smiled weakly.

I kept my head down and pretended to rinse out the sink but really I was washing my hands under the hot water. The water was so scalding that I thought it'd strip my skin off right down to the bone. I had to do it because I'd touched the mole and now all I could think about was the woman's germs on me, infecting me. In fact, I thought of it all afternoon: the small piece of blancmange resting on top of her head. I was so traumatised that when a friend suggested going out to the pub later that evening, I jumped at the chance. I was only 16, but with the amount of makeup I wore, a tight fitting dress, and pair of high heels, I easily passed for 18. However, unbeknown to me, I'd been spotted by another stylist so, the following day when I rang in sick, the manageress knew she'd rumbled me.

'I've got a blister, on my foot it's killing me,' I told her.

She wasn't impressed.

'Wear a pair of trainers then.'

'No way!' I squealed.

She knew I was lying about the blister and was convinced I was hung-over. I wasn't but I couldn't tell her the real reason why.

'Come in on Monday,' she said abruptly. 'I need to speak to you.'

My heart pounded as she slammed the phone down but I couldn't blame her. I was hardly employee of the month! I'd bunked off and I'd only been there a week! When I arrived on Monday morning, I was given a full week's wage of £68, and my notice. As I looked at the wage in my hands I realised just how peeled my skin had become. I'd taken it off layer by layer, not through hairdressing but through constant hand washing. My compulsion had begun to damage me in more ways than one.

'Are you not in work today?' Mum asked the following morning when she passed me in the front room.

'No, not today, it's my day off.'

But the following day she asked the same thing.

'Are you sure you're not in again today?'

I rolled my eyes and threw down a magazine.

'God, what is this, twenty questions?'

By the third day, I was running out of excuses so I decided to come clean. To be honest, I wasn't disappointed when I'd got the sack, all I felt was pure relief because I'd never have to step foot inside the salon again.

'I just didn't like it there Mum. You don't know what it was like,' I said trying to find the right words.

But she wasn't impressed and rightly so.

'Well, you'll have to find a proper job then. You're not hanging around here all day.'

I didn't tell Mum about the old lady, the mole, or my obsession with germs because I thought she'd think I was mad. Instead I tried my best to find another job. I was absolutely thrilled when I did. Unlike the last place, this position had prospects so Mum was delighted too. I'd be a personal assistant to two directors working at a firm of mortgage brokers. The office was busy and I'd share my part of it with two colleagues called David and Claire. I liked them both instantly but Claire especially was a sweet girl. She was meant to be my boss but we soon became good friends. Claire was older than me, in her early twenties, and she was responsible for filing, photocopying and faxing documents. My job was to book accommodation and flights for the two directors. I also had to organise the office Christmas party, which I loved because it meant sorting everything right down to the last detail. The company mostly arranged mortgages and wills for customers. I loved it there because it fulfilled my need to arrange things and keep them in order, to the point of precision. As the months passed by, the more I excelled. The firm even offered to pay for me to study for an NVQ and, every Tuesday, Claire and I would travel to a unit on an industrial estate in East Grinstead to take the course together. Despite my lack of qualifications, I knew it was a step up the ladder: a real chance for me to better myself. I learned how to use the office computer software and was trusted to meet and greet important clients when they arrived at the office. In fact,

I was so busy posting, faxing and filing that I didn't have as much spare time to wash my hands. However, I still found the time to nip off to the toilets so I could apply my makeup. Sometimes, if it was really quiet, I'd even sit and put it on at my desk.

'Here, don't let them catch you doing that,' Claire said one day as I slicked my lashes with a third coat of mascara.

'Oh, I'll be okay, just keep an eye out will you, in case one of them comes in?'

'What are you like, Hayley?' she laughed as she watched the door.

Claire was such a lovely person she didn't think it odd that I applied my makeup every hour of every day. She didn't see the bad in anyone.

But my makeup paled into insignificance because now I was on a new quest: to get tanned. To me, having darker skin meant I'd look and feel skinnier. As luck would have it I was invited on a girls' holiday by my best friend Lucy. She asked me to go to Kos in Greece, with her and a bunch of other girls. In total, there were six of us. I couldn't wait because it was my first holiday abroad without my family. More importantly, I knew I'd have the chance to lounge about on a beach topping up my tan – the thought of getting brown calmed me because to me, sunbathing was the best bit. I packed my suitcase but didn't bother including sun tan lotion because I knew it'd stop me getting brown. Instead I packed some 'tingle cream'. The cream itched and tingled against my skin, bringing the blood to the surface, which gave me an even deeper tan. It contained absolutely no sun block which was fine by me because I wanted to get as brown as possible.

As soon as we arrived I headed straight to the beach. I laid there from 7am until 5pm every day, without fail. It didn't matter if we'd all been up until the early hours the night before because nothing would keep me away. In reality, I'd just swapped the sun bed for a sun lounger but now I had the real thing I was determined to make the most of it. If anything, I longed to be browner because I knew as soon as I stepped off the plane, my tan would start to fade and the thought of looking pale made me feel nauseous. I was young, free and single so I had the time to feed my obsession. No one asked or really cared why I spent every day lying on the beach. I didn't think I had a problem because Lucy was as hardcore as me so I thought it was normal behaviour. In many ways it was but, unlike Lucy, mine wasn't so much a desire to get tanned as a compulsion.

I didn't realise it then but this holiday would change everything because, unbeknown to me, I was about to meet the man I'd spend the rest of my life with.

COMING
CLEAN
LIVING WITH OCD

**CHAPTER 7**

# *MEETING ROB*

THE BEACH WAS glorious and I couldn't get enough of it. 'What do you think, Hayley? Shall we stay for a little longer?' Lucy asked.

I shielded a hand against my eyes and looked up at the blistering sun, still high in the sky. There were still a few more hours before it went down.

'Just another hour, then we'll be done.'

Lucy smiled because she knew what I was like. Still, I felt I couldn't tell her or anyone else my secret: that I didn't just *want* to sit on the beach, I *needed* to be there because I *needed* my skin to be as dark as possible. It was a few more hours before the sun finally began to sink behind the horizon and that's when I admitted defeat. I packed up my things and returned to the hotel. We had three rooms between us, with two girls in each. I shared with a girl called Jodie. Our room was a hub of excitement as we washed, blow dried and straightened our hair, all vying for space in front of the mirror. As usual, I took ages to get ready because, whatever I did, I just didn't look quite right.

'Come on,' one of the girls nagged as they headed for the door. 'We need to go.'

But I wasn't happy so I applied more foundation and topped up my lipstick. Finally, after hours of pampering, I was ready to face the world.

'What's she like, eh?' Lucy grinned as we headed out of the hotel for a night on the town.

Kos was buzzing with hundreds of people spilling out of and milling around neon lit bars. Dance music thumped out of them as we tried to make our minds up about where to start.

'Here, let's try this one. We haven't been in here yet,' one of the girls suggested, pointing towards the door of a club.

The music sounded really loud standing outside on the street so we decided to give it a go. Sure enough, with the alcohol flowing and music thumping, the place was packed. I was with Lucy on the dance floor when one of the other girls frantically beckoned me over with her hand. She was standing at the bar speaking to two boys but one in particular was looking straight at me.

'Hayley,' she called. 'Come here.'

Even though I'd had a drink, I still felt a little unsure of myself. My friend saw me hesitate and walked over, grabbing my hand.

'Come over here, I'm chatting to this guy and I want you to meet his friend.'

I looked over at him and blushed when I realised he was still looking at me. I took him in, his lovely face and hair, his pale blue shirt, his jeans and cool Diesel trainers. He looked good: clean and well dressed – and he had the cutest smile.

'Hi, I'm Rob,' he said.

'Hayley,' I grinned.

I felt unsure of myself so I looked down at my empty glass. Rob noticed I didn't have a drink and turned back to the bar to order me one.

'What are you drinking?'

'Malibu and pineapple.'

He grinned and called the barman over.

With his back turned I was able to look in more detail. *He was lovely!* I looked at my mate and grinned to let her know she'd done well: Rob was just my type. I'd had a few boyfriends at school but nothing serious. Usually, I'd go out with a boy one week but finish with him the next so my love life had been pretty uneventful, until now. As soon as Rob and I started to talk I liked him instantly. He had an uncanny ability to put me at ease and he was also really funny so, when he went to kiss me at the end of the night, I let him.

'Can I see you tomorrow?' he asked, as we wandered back to the hotel.

I nodded.

'Great, I'll take you out for lunch.'

My stomach turned. Lunch meant food. Eating food in a restaurant, in front of strangers and in front of Rob! Although I'd felt comfortable with him, I'd had a few drinks so my guard was down. Being stone cold sober with a meal was an entirely different matter.

'Okay,' I replied weakly.

After he'd left, I started to worry. I'd have to think of something. I'd have to get out of lunch. The following morning I looked at my watch. It was almost 6.30am: I was missing valuable beach time. Tip-toeing quietly around the others, I gathered up my things, a towel and tingle cream, and headed straight for the beach. It was deserted so I chose a good spot and settled down for the day. Within a few hours it started to fill up. Lucy joined me and later we nipped back to the hotel.

'Lunch?' Rob asked, tapping lightly at my hotel door.

I smiled as I opened it even though I had no appetite. I felt sick but I didn't want to say no because I really liked him.

'So, where do you want to go?' he asked as we strolled into town.

My mind whirred because I didn't know what to say. I really liked Rob but I knew I'd have to eat in front of him and he'd see how ugly I was – then he'd run a mile!

*What if I spilled food on my chin? What would I look like when I ate my food?*

All these irrational thoughts raced through my mind as we walked towards the old town. The closer the restaurants got, the more my heart thudded and my palms began to sweat. I had to think of something – quick!

'There's a nice little Greek restaurant we could go to...' I suggested, my voice trailing off.

The last thing I wanted was a plate of food but I knew I'd have to go along with it otherwise Rob would think I didn't like him. Also, I reasoned, it was better to go somewhere I'd been before because it'd be less daunting.

'Okay,' he agreed. 'Show me where it is and we'll head there.'

I knew the restaurant well although I'd never eaten a full meal there; I'd just pushed it around my plate. A few nights before, the holiday rep had noticed and asked why I wasn't eating my lasagne. I was startled because I hadn't thought anyone had realised but he had and he wanted to know why.

'Because it's disgusting,' I lied.

He rolled his eyes.

'No, it's not. It's you; you're just a fussy eater!'

I'd laughed it off as a joke but it wasn't funny because I'd hardly eaten a thing all holiday. Instead, I'd snacked on crisps and nibbles throughout the day.

The restaurant was cool inside. The air conditioning worked hard against the stifling heat. The staff knew me well and smiled with recognition as soon as I walked in through the door. I'd spent most nights in there laughing and drinking with the other girls. The staff had lapped it up, nicknaming us the 'Spice Girls'.

'Hey, Hayley!' one of the waiters called over as soon as he spotted me.

He ushered us to a table and flashed me a cheeky grin as he handed over some menus.

'Boyfriend?' he asked, giving Rob a sly wink.

'Nah,' I replied flushing bright red. 'No, he's not my boyfriend, he's just a friend.'

Rob blushed before covering his face with the menu. I hid too because I needed to buy extra time. I really liked Rob but the last thing I wanted to do was eat a meal in front of him. There was something else too, I felt a little sick because I fancied him. I tried to focus on the menu and choose something light which I wouldn't eat.

'I'll have the chicken Caesar salad,' I decided.

The waiter nodded and turned to Rob.

'And for you?'

'I'll have the same.'

As Rob handed his menu back I noticed his hand tremble

slightly. It made me feel better because I realised he was as nervous as me. Still, despite our nerves, the conversation flowed and we chatted about everything from music to which bars we'd been to.

'So, how long are you here for?' he asked, taking a swig of his beer.

'It's my first week. How about you?'

'It's my last week. Only a few more days to go,' he said pulling a sad face.

My heart sank. I'd hoped Rob was there at the same time as me but in a few days he'd be gone. However, there was some good news. It turned out he lived in Croydon, just up the motorway from me. He was 23, a few years older than me, and had two brothers and a sister. Also, he still lived at home with his mum and dad.

By the time the food arrived, nerves got the better of me and I spent the whole time pushing my salad around the plate with a fork. I messed it up until it had looked as though I'd eaten something. Rob was also nervous and did the same. The waiter seemed a little offended when he collected our plates.

'The food was good, no?' he asked.

'Yes, it was lovely, I'm just not hungry.'

'Me neither,' Rob agreed.

I took his nerves as a good sign because I hoped it meant he liked me as much as I did him. He was different to other boys because he was charming, funny and with lots of banter. He was so friendly that, after only a few hours together, I felt as though I'd known him for years. So, when he asked me out later that night I readily agreed although my face fell when he suggested going out for dinner! It felt like double torture because I knew I couldn't get away with not eating in front of him twice in one day. As it happened, I engineered it so we didn't end up going out at all. Instead, we wandered around with Rob suggesting every restaurant in Kos.

'How about here?' he said pointing towards an idyllic Greek taverna by the sea.

I shook my head.

'Nah, I don't like the look of it.'

'Here?'

I refused.

'No, it's too close to those!' I said pointing towards some overflowing bins

The truth was, it wasn't the restaurant or the bins: it was me. My stomach was all churned up inside as we passed Greek, English, Chinese even Indian restaurants.

'Here?'

'Nah, I don't like that type of food,' I added.

I used every trick in the book to stop us from having to sit down and order a meal. Rob sighed. He'd been patient but now he was fast running out of options.

'Well, why don't we just go back to the place we went earlier?'

I grabbed his hand and turned to face him.

'Are you really hungry? I mean, *really* hungry?' I asked.

Rob shrugged his shoulders as if he didn't care.

'It's just I'm not hungry, not anymore.'

Rob grinned. He seemed relieved; I think he was worried I didn't want to go for a meal with him. I didn't, but it was nothing to do with him and everything to do with food.

'So, do you just want to go for a drink then?'

I nodded, glad that we'd get to spend time together without having to eat in public. Shortly afterwards, we were standing inside a bar when I noticed something. Rob was almost perfect but there was one thing puzzling me. If he'd been there for almost two weeks then why on earth was he so pale? It didn't make sense. After a few more drinks I decided to ask.

'So,' I began, the music was loud which made it hard to hear but I had to ask him the one thing which had been bugging me. 'Don't you tan?'

Rob smirked and pretended to look himself up and down. 'Yeah,' he laughed, 'why?'

'But you look so...' I waved my hand around trying to search for the right word. 'You look so... pale and pasty. I mean, you look so pale... to say you've been out here for two weeks.' I took a huge gulp of my drink for courage.

'I bet I go darker than you, darling!' He laughed, a wicked grin across his face.

*He had to be joking. I was the queen of tans!*

'No you don't!' I replied giving him a playful push.

'Yes, I do! I go loads darker than you!'

I looked at him and shook my head. He was one of the palest boys I'd ever seen which made his claim even more ridiculous.

'No you don't,' I retorted.

'Do!'

I laughed because somehow it'd turned into the battle of the tanning!

Rob held up his arms as if to make a point. 'One hundred per cent, I go darker than you.'

I shook my head again; this had to be a wind up.

'Okay, so why are you so pale then? Don't you sunbathe?'

Rob explained that he and his mates had spent pretty much the whole of the two weeks having a good time in all the bars and clubs, leaving little time for the beach. Most nights they didn't even get to bed until 6am.

'Then we don't wake up until 1 or 2pm, so we just go down to the pool for an hour before going back up to the room to get changed for another night out.'

I was appalled.

'But you've missed the best part of the sun!' I gasped.

Rob shrugged as if he didn't care.

'You're missing the sun!' I told him. 'It's hottest around midday so, you're missing the best bit!'

'Yeah,' he grinned. 'But it doesn't matter cos I'm not like you – you're hardcore!'

I held up my arm next to his, he was right. We couldn't be more opposite if we tried, yet there was something about him I really liked. In the end we went on a few more dates but soon it was time for him to fly home. On his last night in Kos, me and the girls decided to go on an 18–30s pub crawl. We knocked back strong booze in every bar, drinking something called a fishbowl – a potent cocktail in a huge glass with six straws sticking out of it. I was so drunk that I soon forgot about my obsession with germs and agreed to share along with everyone else. It felt good to have a night off from my fears. By the time we'd reached the final pub, the night was in full swing. To be honest, we were all shot to shit. The girls were wearing T-shirts given to us by one of the bars on the pub crawl. I was also wearing a pair of cropped denim shorts so, when the DJ in the bar set a challenge I was straight on it.

'The first girl up here wearing a pair of men's boxer shorts wins a prize!' His voice boomed.

My eyes scanned the room with determination and that's when I saw him – a granddad sitting with his wife and grandkids having a quiet drink at the side of the room. As soon as I approached he started to laugh and entered into the full spirit of things, pulling off the pair of shorts he was wearing. He saw my face and started to chuckle.

'Don't worry love, I've got a spare pair on underneath.'

I couldn't believe I was doing it but with my mates egging me on, I pulled the old fella's pants up over the top of my own shorts, jumped on a nearby table and started to dance. I was being a total show off – the complete opposite of who I usually was. I won another fishbowl cocktail to share with the girls who, by now, were dancing on the table with me. I didn't care, I was having fun, letting my hair down for once and it felt good. For the first time in ages my inhibitions melted away and I felt amazing. It'd been the 'Rob effect'. He'd done this to me; this guy had somehow managed to bring out the best in me and allowed me to feel normal. For the first time in my whole life I didn't give a shit what people thought of me. Soon, I was so pissed that I could hardly stand up straight. Afterwards, we stumbled into the Aussie bar where Rob was drinking with his mates. I decided to keep my prize boxer shorts on, a present from the old bloke in the bar, because by now, I was past caring.

'Who's your mate, Rob?' his friends jeered as soon as I walked into the bar with the boxers over my shorts.

They all cheered but Rob just laughed it off.

'Yeah, she's with me,' he admitted throwing his head in his hands dramatically.

I laughed along too because I loved him more in that moment. I knew then that Rob was just the man for a crazy bird like me.

'What?' I asked as I approached.

'Err, those.' He pointed down at the boxer shorts.

'It's not what it looks like,' I explained as I told Rob all about the challenge and the old man taking his pants off.

'Don't worry, he had another pair on underneath!' I giggled, putting a hand to my chest.

'What are you like?'

The following day, when Rob left for the airport I called around to say goodbye. He offered me his telephone number but I didn't want to look needy, like a desperate girl chasing a boy, so I gave him my number instead. I wasn't sure if he'd ring but I hoped he would.

'I'll call you,' he promised. 'Have a nice week. And Hayley,' he said turning back towards me. 'Don't get too brown!'

It made me laugh.

'You're just jealous because you're so white and pasty!'

Rob raised a hand to wave goodbye.

'Just cos you're so hardcore!' he retaliated.

After he'd left, I felt a little lost. I enjoyed the rest of the holiday but without Rob it just wasn't as much fun.

'He was nice,' one of the girls said later on the beach.

I was lost in my own thoughts, thinking about Rob and she must have sensed it.

'Thanks,' I replied. 'He is nice. He's really nice.'

The final week passed by in a blur of drinks, dancing and being chatted up. I thought of Rob, but I was only 17 years old and I convinced myself that it'd just been a holiday romance. Deep down, I thought I'd never see or hear from him again. So, when I was home from holiday, I ignored the phone when it rang.

'Hayley,' Mum called. 'There's someone on the phone for you.'

'Who is it?' I asked.

I'd just got out of the shower and my hair was dripping wet.

'It's Rob.'

I pulled the towel away from my head – I couldn't hear her properly.

'Who?'

'Rob,' she repeated.

'Rob who?'

'Oh, I don't know! Why don't you come and answer it then you can ask him?'

I picked up the phone.

'Hello,' my voice sounded cautious.

*It couldn't be Rob, not my Rob.*

'Hi,' the man replied. 'It's Rob.'

'Rob who?'

'Rob from holiday.'

My heart lifted as the penny dropped and I felt a little bit stupid. Of course it was Rob. He was the only Rob I knew who'd said he'd call.

'Oh, hi!' I said sounding a little surprised.

'So, you know who I am now?'

'Yeah, yeah, sorry, I was just. I mean, I think I'm still a little bit tired from the flight.'

Rob chuckled as he listened to my excuses.

'So, did you have a good time?'

'Yeah, great.'

'And you're not too brown?'

'Yeah, course I am!' I giggled.

We started chatting and it was as though we'd never been apart so, when Rob asked me out on a date the following day, I readily agreed.

'Great, listen, I'll come and get you in my new car because I pick it up tomorrow.'

'Ooh, what kind of car is it?' I asked.

My mind raced with flash images of Mercedes, Audi or even a BMW.

'It's a new Mini Cooper,' Rob replied, as proud as punch.

'A Mini?' I screeched.

Suddenly the bubble burst. A Mini drove into my mind, until all I could think of was Rob driving a bright yellow Mini like Mr Bean off the bloody TV!

## CHAPTER 8

# *HIDING IN ROB'S ROOM*

'WELL, WHAT DO you think?' Rob grinned widely as he led me outside to show me his new car.

I breathed with relief; at least it wasn't bright yellow! Instead it was black, white and small, very small.

'Is this it?' was all I could muster.

I opened up the passenger door and climbed inside. Rob turned the key in the ignition and we set off, back to his house. As we whizzed along the road Rob turned to face me.

'Well,' he said.

I wasn't sure what he meant so I pulled a puzzled face.

'Well, what?'

'What do you think of her? Even if you don't like Minis you have to admit she's a lovely car.'

I shrugged. I knew Rob had waited over nine months for it but, try as I might; I wasn't too fussed about his new motor.

'It's a bit like a Mr Bean car,' I blurted out without thinking.

Rob's eyes shot around to face me with an expression of pure horror.

'Mr Bean?'

'Yeah, you know, he drives one of these things, doesn't he? At least yours isn't bright yellow though!' I laughed but Rob was having none of it.

'Mr Bean, is that what you think? But Minis are cool! They're like what everyone wants right now. I can't believe you're slating my car. I've waited nine months for this!' he gasped, tapping the steering wheel with the palm of his hand.

'It is better in black and white, I have to admit.'

'I should think so. Look at the dashboard and the controls. Look at the interior!' Rob said tapping the roof with his hand as if to make a point. 'Every little space is so well designed.'

'It's alright, I suppose.'

'Alright?'

'Yeah, well, it's not exactly rocking my world, that's for sure,' I added sarcastically.

Without warning, Rob indicated and pulled over at the side of the road. Traffic whizzed past as the car came to an abrupt halt and he pulled on the handbrake.

'Right,' he said waving his hand over at me, 'Get out!'

My heart began to thud.

*What did he mean? Was he really throwing me out in the middle of nowhere?*

'I didn't mean to… I mean I wasn't being…'

A wicked grin broke across Rob's face and that's when I realised he was winding me up.

'I had you going for a minute, didn't I?' he said laughing and nudging me with his left elbow.

I shook my head and burst out laughing because it was true, I'd believed every word!

That night, we arranged to go back to Rob's house for the evening. I felt fresh and revived because I had a lovely deep tan. To me, having a tan meant I looked and felt so much better. It gave me confidence which was good because I didn't have a clue what was in store for me. As soon we walked into Rob's house the chaos of the place hit me. I knew it was partly my problem – I was a neat freak – but Rob's family home was cluttered and messy with nothing in its place. There was no order. I thought back to Mum's house. It was so spotless it looked like a showroom, not a house with four girls living in it. Even our garage had fresh carpet on the floor, but Rob's was the complete opposite. It shocked me. Up until this point, Rob had had a calming effect because when we were together; I stopped obsessing but, right now, standing inside his home, I felt dirty and contaminated as though I wanted to pull my skin off my body. I tried my best not to show my horror and followed Rob into the living room where his mum Kay was sat reading a book on the sofa.

'Hi Mum, this is Hayley, the girl I've been telling you about', he said, introducing me.

Rob's mum looked up momentarily from her book and studied me. By the look on her face I could tell she wasn't very impressed.

'Hi,' she replied weakly before looking straight back down at the open page.

I tried to smile but deep down I was convinced she didn't like me. I felt awkward standing there and glanced down at myself.

*Perhaps it was my clothes?*

I looked at my denim pedal pushers and off the shoulder top. *Maybe she thought I looked too tarty?*

I was anxious because I knew she was judging me. I'd hoped for more than a 'hi'. It was obvious I wasn't the sort of girl she would have picked for her son but I didn't know what to do or say to make her like me. Rob looked at his mum and then at me. He sensed an atmosphere and grabbed my hand.

'Come on, Hayley,' he said, leading me out into the hallway to talk.

I glanced at Kay but she didn't even look up – it made me feel even worse.

'So,' he said wrapping his arm around my waist. 'What do you want to do tonight then?'

If I thought we were having a private conversation then I was sorely mistaken because moments later Kay was at his side.

'You do know its Natalie's 30th birthday party tonight, don't you?' she said, looking at Rob. 'So, we've got plans.'

He held up his hands in protest.

'But I've got Hayley here with me, Mum. She's just got back from Kos.'

Rob's mum turned to face me for the first time. I smiled in the hope she wouldn't be so frosty.

'Ah, that's why you're so brown then!' she quipped.

I knew she was having a dig at me. It was clear she thought I was too tanned. I felt in the middle as Rob and his mum discussed the impending party over the top of me. In a bid to smooth things over I decided to interrupt.

'I don't mind going. Honestly, it'll be nice,' I smiled through gritted teeth.

Rob's mum shot me a look which said she'd only meant Rob, not me.

'Okay, we'll both go,' Rob sighed. He'd done it to keep the peace even though Kay was far from happy.

'Fine,' she said disappearing back into the front room.

'So, who's going to be there?' I asked Rob a little later when we were alone.

'Everyone, I expect.'

My stomach flipped.

*Everyone?*

'What, like all your family?'

'Yep, I expect so.'

I pulled a worried face so Rob took me in his arms and gave me a reassuring cuddle.

'Hey, don't look so scared!' he soothed. 'At least this way you'll get it all over and done with. You'll meet the whole family in one go.'

That was the problem, I thought to myself: all those people, all those strangers judging me.

The closer it got to time for us to leave, the more I panicked. But I knew how important this was to Rob. They were his family so I wanted to make a good impression.

*I mustn't mess this up,* I told myself.

In truth, I didn't really want to go but I also didn't want to rock the boat or cause conflict between Rob and his mum. Yet the other half of me felt as though I was being thrown into the lion's den.

*At least it's not a family meal,* I thought. *At least that's something to be thankful for.*

All too soon it was time to leave.

'I'm just going to put some makeup on,' I said, grabbing my handbag.

'You look fine,' Rob protested.

But I didn't feel fine, I felt terrified. I needed to apply another layer of makeup – my secret mask – to hide how scared I felt inside.

'Where's the bathroom?' I said putting my compact down, 'I need a bigger mirror.'

Rob opened the bedroom door and pointed over towards it. 'Won't be long.'

I immediately went over to the sink to wash my hands. I'd been sat in the house for hours and now I felt dirty.

*I'll be covered in germs, I need to get clean and I need to do it now.*

Grabbing the soap, I started to scrub at my hands and that's when I spotted it out of the corner of my eye – a big blob of spit right in the middle of the sink. It was enough to push me over the edge. I retched as bile rose at the back of my throat. My hands were soapy so I ran over to the toilet where I was violently sick. After a while, the retching subsided and I lifted my head up and away from the toilet bowl. I looked across at the bath and was horrified when I spotted a chalky ring where the water level had been. Then I looked down at the toilet bowl and recoiled with horror.

*I've just had my head in there,* I shuddered, my blood running cold.

I held my hands in mid-air so that I didn't touch anything. Everything felt so dirty. In reality, Kay's home was just like millions of others up and down the country. There was nothing wrong with her house; it was my reaction which was extreme. I had extremely high standards, only I didn't realise. Instead I wondered why everyone wasn't as clean as me.

I rinsed the soap off my hands as I tried not to look at the offending gob nestled in the sink. Once I was certain they were clean, I ran back to the safety of Rob's room. He looked up as soon as I came stumbling in through the door.

'Are you alright?'

My body was trembling but I couldn't tell him the real reason, that I thought his home was horrible and dirty, so I changed the subject.

'Have you got a mirror in here I can use?' I smiled weakly.

After I'd retouched my makeup for the umpteenth time, we set off for Natalie's house. Natalie is Rob's sister-in-law and is married to his brother Colin. When Kay had said it would be a party at his brother's house, that what I assumed it would be, only I was wrong. As soon as we knocked at the front door, Colin answered and we were engulfed in an aroma of curry.

*Why does the house smell of curry?* I wondered.

Colin was lovely and seemed genuinely pleased to meet me, which made me feel a little better. However, as soon as we turned the corner, my worst fears were confirmed. Sitting in long jumbled lines were around a dozen members of Rob's family. To make matters worse, as I followed him inside they all looked up.

'This is Hayley,' Rob said grabbing my hand.

Kay was already there, sitting in a prime spot on the sofa. I wondered if she'd already filled them in on me and my deep tan.

'Hi,' I said pretending to wave a friendly hello, even though the atmosphere felt far from it.

I cringed because I felt so awkward but just when I thought it couldn't get any worse. I spotted something else – numerous dishes full of curry, rice and plates of naan bread and poppadoms.

'You didn't say there'd be food,' I whispered to Rob.

My palms felt clammy as my heart began to race.

'I didn't know,' he whispered back.

I tried my best to socialise, but the food in the corner was freaking me out. I knew I had to escape; I had to think of a reason to leave.

*If I left, then I wouldn't have to eat.*

The room was hot and claustrophobic. The smell of curry mixed with my fear left me nauseous. I caught a few of Rob's family looking over which made me feel worse. Then one of them got up and started helping herself to food: the buffet was open. Everyone followed and I knew I had to escape.

'I need a cig,' I gasped as I rose to my feet, slinging my handbag over my shoulder.

My hands were trembling at the thought of having to eat food in front of so many strangers. I struggled in restaurants never mind a house like this, where I wanted everyone to like me.

It felt cool as I pushed open the back door and stepped out into the garden. The moon cast down an eerie light as I pulled out a cigarette and lit it. But the amber glow and draw of nicotine calmed me as smoke filled my lungs. I knew smoking was a filthy habit but that hadn't stopped me from starting to smoke because I used cigarettes as a prop to stop me from having to eat. Not only did they suppress my appetite, they also allowed me to escape whenever I was faced with an awkward social situation. In short, cigarettes were the best diversion tactic I had.

'You okay?' A voice called from the backdoor.

It was Rob. He stepped into the garden and approached me.

'I'm fine,' I said taking another long drag. I blew out a stream of grey smoke which billowed and disappeared up into the night air, 'I just don't want any food, that's all.'

'Nah, me neither.'

I felt as though someone had lifted a huge weight off my shoulders. If Rob didn't want to eat then it took the pressure off of me.

'Can we leave in a bit?' I asked.

I knew it was wrong to ask because this was Rob's family, not mine, but I also knew I couldn't stay. I thought he might go mad but, if anything, he seemed relieved.

'I'm not bothered about staying,' he admitted.

The truth was, Rob felt as awkward as I did so, in the end, we left the party after only an hour.

'What, you leaving already?' a relative asked as we headed towards the front door.

'Yeah,' Rob grinned.

Suddenly, his youngest brother Ben got up and followed us out into the hallway.

'Please don't go!' he pleaded.

I looked at Rob and back at Ben. It was clear he wanted to escape too.

'You can come with us, if you like?' I offered.

'Are you sure? I mean, will it be okay?'

Rob nodded. Ben was only 17 – the same age as me – he was far too young for family gatherings. We said our goodbyes and left the house. As Ben climbed into the backseat he leaned forward and tapped me on the shoulder.

'Thanks Hayley, I thought I was going to be sat there all night,' he smirked.

I laughed because he was just like Rob – honest and open.

As soon as we arrived back at the house, Ben disappeared off upstairs.

'Shall we order a Chinese takeaway?' Rob suggested as he searched around for a menu.

'I'm not sure I like it,' I said, as quick as a flash.

I had to think of something otherwise I knew Rob would make me eat.

'No, you've got to try a Chinese,' he insisted.

'But I'm not really hungry and...' my voice trailed off because I realised it was no good – I wouldn't be able to get out of this one.

'Listen, I know this really good place, you'll absolutely love it.' He said, refusing to take no for an answer.

'Okay,' I agreed, even though I didn't have a clue how I'd manage to eat it. 'Just don't put too much on my plate when it comes, please.'

I wanted to tell Rob about my phobia of food but something stopped me. I was worried he'd think I was weird and wouldn't want to see me again so I went along with it because I wanted him to think I was 'normal'.

I listened as Rob rang through the order.

'Sweet and sour chicken with special fried rice, please,' he said, reading from the menu.

I stuck up my hand in the air and waved it to get his attention.

'Hang on, wait a minute,' he told the person on the other end of the line.

'Please can you ask them to take the prawns out of the rice because I really don't like them.'

Rob nodded and asked for the prawns to be removed.

'And a chicken chow mein,' he continued.

I waved my hand again. This time Rob took the phone away from his ear.

'Could you ask them to make it without onion or bean sprouts because I hate them too, sorry!' I smiled.

I was being a complete pain in the arse but I knew if all the horrible stuff had been taken out then maybe, just maybe I might be able to eat some of it. Rob nodded his head and repeated my request. After he'd put the phone down he didn't say a word but then, he didn't have to because it was clear he thought I was some stuck up princess! As soon as the takeaway arrived, we took it up to his bedroom so we could eat it in private. It was the moment I'd been dreading but when Rob placed a few things on my plate, something felt different. I felt different because now, right there in that room, it was just Rob and me. I steeled myself, half-expecting to panic but remarkably, I stayed calm. Instead of the usual racing heart and sweaty palms, for the first time I felt in control. More than that, I was able to load up my fork with food and pick at it, eating it in front of this wonderful man. I was completely at ease in his presence and it felt fantastic. Rob wasn't just a familiar face, I trusted him and now I was falling in love with him. He was such a kind person that I couldn't help myself. Just being with him helped me because he was so grounded and 'normal'. Rob liked me too and it was a nice feeling. For the first time in my life, I didn't have to pretend to be someone or something else because Rob liked the real Hayley. Only deep down, the real Hayley was a complicated bundle of worries and right now, the cat hair in his house was freaking me out. It was everywhere, downstairs on the sofa, even on Rob's bed! I loved all animals but my irrational fears convinced me Rob's cats would have fleas.

*If they've got fleas then they'll infect me and make me sick!*

I knew I was being irrational but it was all I could think whenever I saw Kay's cats. She had two: Snoop was a black cat who loved to sneak undetected into Rob's bedroom, while Tweet was a shy black-and-white moggy. Their contrasting colours meant their fur showed up on every surface. With Snoop on the prowl, every time I slipped out to the bathroom, I made sure Rob's bedroom door was closed behind me to stop him from sneaking in. Despite my fear of cats, I stayed the night of the Chinese take away. The following morning, Rob left bright and early to play football with his mates.

'But I don't want you to leave me here.'

'I'll be back by 2pm, just make yourself comfortable. I won't be long, promise,' he said leaning down to kiss me on the forehead.

Kay was downstairs but after leaving the party early, taking Ben with us, I couldn't face her. I was worried she'd already made her mind up about me and now I was too nervous to strike up polite conversation. I was a teenager so, in many ways, I was lacking in confidence. Also, I didn't want to go downstairs because I didn't want to see the state of the kitchen. I knew if it wasn't spotless, it'd send me into a blind panic and this time, I wouldn't be able to hide it. Instead I hid in Rob's bedroom waiting for him to return. To pass the time I decided to sort through his stuff, placing it in neat little piles, but it didn't look right.

*What Rob's bedroom needed was a proper spring clean and a thorough clear-out. It was a total mess, but I'd soon sort it out for him!*

I knew exactly what needed to be done: I had to shift his furniture. Like the little girl of ten years before, I pushed and pulled stuff around until I felt completely happy. Looking back, poor Kay must have wondered who her son had brought home – a young girl too scared to come downstairs but bold enough to rearrange her son's bedroom when he wasn't even there. It took me a while, but where once everything had been unacceptable and messy, now there was perfect order and symmetry.

*Rob's going to love it!* I thought happily to myself.

As I proudly surveyed the room, my mobile phone bleeped on the top of the bed. It was Rob; he'd sent me a text. I smiled as I clicked it open and began to read.

*Are u ok?* It read. *What are u doing? Mum says there's been loads of noise coming from upstairs. She said you've been moving stuff around.*

I froze to the spot and looked at the floor beneath my feet. I hadn't realised but I'd made such a racket that Kay had heard downstairs and had called Rob to tell on me. God only knows what she'd think about me now!

*Maybe I've gone too far?*

My fears were confirmed when Rob came home with a puzzled look on his face. Needless to say, I could tell what he was thinking: *What the hell has this girl done to my bedroom?*

'What have you done?' he gasped, his eyes scanning the room.

'Don't you like it?' I replied a little disappointed.

'Yeah, err, it's just...' he said struggling to find the right words.

But I was certain once he'd looked properly, he'd be really pleased with everything.

'I've put a lot of your stuff in here,' I said opening up the top of a bin bag to show him. I'd filled it up with his things and wedged it into a corner of the room.

'So if you can't find something, then look in here,' I continued.

But Rob wasn't listening; instead he was turning around taking in the changes – all the stuff I'd cleared away and removed from his childhood bedroom.

'You don't like it, do you?' I sighed, letting go of the bin liner.

'No, no, it's not that – it looks really good,' he replied but his face said it all. His face said: *She can go home tonight and never come back. She's crazy, this one*!

Despite my uninvited attempts to sort out his bedroom, Rob let me stay on Saturday night too. He finally dropped me back home at Mum's house on Sunday afternoon and kissed me goodbye. If he thought I was mental, he didn't say it. Although I didn't even realise I'd done anything wrong.

## CHAPTER 9

# BURNING SKIN

I WAS STILL happy in my job as PA, when a few weeks later a friend of Lauren's called at our house. She worked at a nearby tanning salon and mentioned there was a job going there. As soon as I heard, my ears pricked up.

'Are they looking for someone now?'

'Yeah, there's a job. Why, do you want it?'

A rush of excitement flooded through me.

'I'd love it! Why, would you be able to put a word in for me?'

'Course, no problem!' she replied and she did.

Within days I'd not only had an interview, I'd been given the position. I was so excited that I couldn't wait to tell Rob. Although he was happy for me, he was also a little concerned.

'Are you sure, Hayley?'

But I was adamant.

'It's what I want,' I insisted and it was.

Even though my office job had better prospects, the thought of working in a tanning salon seemed so much more exciting because there were lots of benefits to be had. For starters, I'd be able to use the sun beds. In my head, using the sun beds meant I'd get darker and, if I was darker, I'd look thinner. Soon, all I could see were positives and no negatives. Although I was earning a good wage, my obsession with how I looked was paramount until it was all-consuming. I knew I was sabotaging my own career but I didn't care. Working in a tanning salon made perfect sense. It'd free up more time to improve the way I looked and the way I felt about myself – in short it was my perfect job. Of course, my bosses were disappointed when I handed in my notice, but Claire wished me luck because she knew how much it meant to me. My lovely colleague even organised a collection and bought me lots of nice presents. I was so overwhelmed that I cried when we finally said goodbye.

'I'm going to miss you,' I wept and I meant it, every single word.

'Me too,' Claire sobbed, giving me a hug.

But Claire wasn't half as gutted as Mum was when I told her what I'd done.

'A tanning salon?' she shrieked. 'You're giving up a good job to work in a tanning salon? You must be mad!'

But I didn't care. Access to five sun beds beat a good job with prospects, hands down.

'I can't believe you're throwing a good job in to work in a poxy sun bed shop,' Mum tutted, shaking her head in despair.

She wouldn't let it go and begged me to reconsider but I ignored her and everyone else. I was 17 years old and I thought I knew better. This was my life and I was free to do whatever I wanted and right now, my heart was telling me to grab this new job with both hands. Besides, what wasn't to like? Working in a sun bed shop meant I'd have lots of time to look better, thinner, and to achieve the tan of my dreams. It was almost too good to be true. In fact, it hardly felt like a job at all! So, only a month after my dream holiday, I began my new position and vowed to top up my fading tan.

'This is where we keep the creams and the sun beds are just through the back here.'

The manageress held out her arm as she gave me a guided tour around the sun bed salon. At the interview she'd asked how soon I could start.

'Next week?' I replied.

I think she was a little taken aback by my enthusiastic response but that's exactly what I did – walked out of one job and straight into another.

The salon was owned by two men but run by the manageress. Between us, we took it in turns to work shifts, often crossing our hours over. Usually, she worked during the daytime and I'd cover the 3pm until 9pm shift. It was ideal because I was entrusted to lock up, which meant I was on my own and had access to the sun beds. There were five in total; a stand-up tanning booth and four lay-down sun beds. Initially I was surprised because there was more to tanning than I'd anticipated and lots of responsibility which went with it. I sat on the front reception desk and it was my job to monitor clients coming through. Most importantly, I had to set the timer for the client using the sun beds. Those with fair skin were allowed between four and six minutes, while clients with darker skin were allowed up to a maximum of ten to twelve, but no one was ever allowed more than twelve minutes. It was up to me to set the timer through a central computer control system on the front desk. I'd set each to the correct time and once that time was up, the sun bed would automatically shut down. It was an important job because without fail, no one was allowed to go longer than their designated time. No one, that is, apart from me. During my lunch hour I'd close the shop and lock the front door but I wouldn't go into town to buy a sandwich. Instead, I'd turn the sign to 'closed', set the sun bed to the maximum 12 minutes and bask in its halogen rays. The computer would only allow 12 minutes so, when my time was up, I'd get off the bed, throw on some clothes, walk back through to the front of the shop and re-set it for another session. I'd read about skin cancer and the possible links to sun beds but to be honest, like most young girls, I hadn't given it a second thought. In a bid to enhance my tan I even used special tingle creams which heightened the response and the colour of your skin.

My job was to book people in and to show them through to their sun bed. It was boring and monotonous work and, sometimes, I'd long to be back in the office because at least there I had less time to focus on myself and my obsessions. Now I'd watch the clock, waiting for lunch so I could have a go on the sun beds. But soon the set 12 minutes didn't feel anywhere close to long enough, so I'd re-set it and then re-set a few more times until soon I was spending up to 45 minutes on them. My skin felt hot and itchy but pain was good because pain and discomfort were feeding my new obsession to be darker. The darker I became, the better I felt. By now, I didn't just *want* it but I *needed* to burn my natural olive skin to the shade of wood. The need to become browner occupied my thoughts until soon it was all I could think of. When the customers were in, I'd sit on the front desk watching the clock waiting for my time on the beds. I was still washing my hands and applying makeup but now I was damaging and prematurely ageing my skin in my quest to be 'perfect'. The darker I became, the better I felt. I convinced myself that darker skin would make me look thinner – like a flattering pair of tight black jeans, only this time I'd wear the same colour from head to toe. After all, black clothes made you look slimmer, so why wouldn't dark skin? It made complete sense. As an added bonus, the darker I became, the whiter my teeth looked. Sometimes the tingle cream would itch against my parched skin but I'd ride through the pain because nothing could or would stop me. I had to have the darkest tan because brown was beautiful and pale and pasty wasn't. I became the opposite of Michael Jackson. Soon, even 45 minutes wasn't enough and I'd spend as long as I dared on the sun bed before the next client arrived. Stupidly, I didn't care about the risks because as long as I was brown then everything would be okay. Even the warmth of the sun bed made me feel better. It was as though I was healing myself by changing my appearance, slowly melting away the old Hayley to make way for the new. Sometimes I'd spend so long laying on them that afterwards, my skin would smell of burning flesh. It was so strong that other people could smell it on me. It should have been my wakeup call but strangely, the smell reassured me because I knew if I smelled then the changes were happening and my skin was getting darker. In fact, I became so brown that I had to change my foundation to match the colour of my body. Now, whenever I applied my old foundation, my face looked like a ghost. Undeterred, I called into a department store to ask for advice. When I showed the sales assistant my original tube of foundation she seemed a little surprised.

'It's four or five shades lighter than your actual skin colour. You'll need to use something much darker.'

Then it was my turn to be shocked because the foundation colour she recommended was one used on Asian skin.

'Really?' I asked.

The girl insisted. Sure enough, she was right.

Most nights Rob would finish work and drive down from Crystal Palace to see me. He'd sit and wait until my shift ended and then we'd drive all the way back to his house so that we could spend the night together. But his mum didn't approve.

'I don't like you driving all that way,' she nagged.

Rob shrugged off her concerns because we were in love. But soon even he started to make comments on my tan.

'Give me your arm,' he asked one morning.

We were lying in bed so I held out my arm, as I did, Rob took it in his hands, held it up to his nose and sniffed.

'I thought I could smell something, it's you,' he said. 'Can't you smell that?'

I lifted my forearm and gave it a quick sniff but I couldn't smell a thing.

'No.'

Rob shook his head and gave my arm another sniff.

'Really, can't you smell that, Hayley?' he asked a little taken aback. 'It smells like something's burning. You smell of burning skin!'

But I couldn't smell it because I was so used to it. If anything all his comments did were make me feel a little more self-conscious. Instead, I sprayed Chanel perfume over myself to mask it. Although I couldn't smell it, I didn't mind the fact I smelled burnt because at least I knew it was working: the sun beds were doing their job. I was there in my own perfect world where I was able to feed my unhealthy obsession every single day without question or argument. My family noticed I was getting darker, yet no matter what anyone said, no one could convince me otherwise – brown was best. At work I was largely on my own so there was no one to tell me what I could or couldn't do. I was inside my own little bubble. I had the perfect job – a little bit of work and a great tan. That was until one day, six months later, when I was told the shop would be closing for good. Fewer and fewer clients were coming through the door because something new had hit the high street – something with less risk, something called a St Tropez spray tan. Also, sun beds had had lots of bad press and people were nervous about using them.

'Looks like we'll be closing in a month so you'll have to look for a new job,' the manageress said glumly.

I was gutted because I knew no job meant no tan – that's how obsessed I was. At first I fretted. My tan was fading by the day and I was getting lighter and so, in my book, I looked fatter and uglier. Instead I switched to St Tropez so, instead of looking brown, I now looked orange! I was a fake and instead of burning my skin I was colouring it in. Somehow, being browner made me feel cleaner, stronger and more in control. My world had to be perfect and it would be as long as I could indulge in my obsessions. I didn't even recognise that I had a problem because makeup, tanning, cleaning and rearranging my world had become a normal way of life to me.

COMING
CLEAN
LIVING WITH OCD

## CHAPTER 10

# *REARRANGING SOMEONE ELSE'S LIFE*

'DON'T LET THAT cat in here!' I shrieked.

We were lying in Rob's bed but I was convinced Snoop would do his usual and try and sneak in when I wasn't looking. By now it'd become a battle of wits, me against Snoop and so far, I'd won!

With my job at the sun bed shop coming to an end I was spending more and more time at Rob's house. But the cats would set me on edge because I was terrified of fleas and of getting sick. One day, Snoop silently snuck in around the corner of the door but I didn't notice. I didn't even feel him as he padded along the top of Rob's duvet, or when he made himself comfortable at the end of the bed, nesting down at the side of my feet. It was only when Rob actually climbed back into bed that Snoop shifted slightly. That's when I spotted him and all hell broke loose.

'Arrghhh!' I shouted. 'Get that cat out of here!'

'Bloody hell Hayley, it's only a cat,' Rob said, trying to calm me down.

But it was no good – I was hysterical. I grabbed the duvet and pulled it close against my eyes because I couldn't look at it.

*What if a flea has jumped off Snoop and onto me? What if it bites me, then I'll get sick and have to go to hospital.* The voice warned.

I knew it was totally irrational but I couldn't help myself.

'He must have sneaked in when I nipped out to the loo,' Rob said as he tried to shoo Snoop back out through the bedroom door. I buried my face underneath the covers, I couldn't bear to watch in case he came back, but then I heard Rob close the door.

'Blimey, you must be really frightened of cats to act like that,' he said climbing back into bed.

'Yeah, something like that,' my voice sounded muffled underneath the duvet and I was boiling hot but I refused to resurface until the coast was clear.

'Has it gone yet?'

'Yes, you can come out now.'

I pulled the duvet from my face and took a deep breath.

'Well, thank God for that!'

'Are you really that scared of cats?' Rob asked. A wicked grin spread across his face because he'd just realised I was completely nuts!

I nodded. 'I hate them.'

It wasn't a lie – I hated cats, only I didn't tell him the real reason why. Afterwards, Rob was meticulous when it came to shutting the door. I don't think Snoop liked me very much; but then again, the feeling was mutual.

There was another cat called Tweet, but thankfully, she preferred to spend her time outdoors. It was a good job because one morning she gave birth to a litter inside the family garage. I was appalled – I thought how filthy it must be and, when Rob showed me around, I realised I was right. Rob's garage was crammed full of old wardrobes and drawers. It was so cluttered that they had to climb over the furniture just to reach Tweet and her kittens. In the end, they gave the kittens away and then, tragically, Tweet was knocked over by a car. I felt sad for Rob and Kay, even though I didn't like cats. Still, Tweet's absence meant the cat hair lessened a little. Even though she'd mostly been an outside cat, she'd still left her mark. It made life at Rob's house a little more bearable, but I still showered every day, sometimes twice, to rid myself of germs. I'd obsessively scrub my body, starting at my toes, working upwards. I just couldn't get clean enough.

Not long afterwards, Rob's mum and dad booked a holiday abroad so, apart from Ben, we had the place to ourselves. I was thrilled because it meant I'd be able to relax with Kay out of the way. I finished my job at the sun bed shop and started to apply for other positions. With time on my hands, my penchant for moving furniture heightened until soon I was tackling more than just Rob's bedroom. With Kay away on holiday, I ventured into the kitchen and was astounded by what I saw – all the tins were mixed up and in no particular order in the cupboards. Some of the labels faced the wrong way. I was absolutely appalled – everything needed a proper Hayley sort out!

'Right,' I said as I snapped on a pair of rubber gloves, 'I'll soon put this in order!'

With Rob at work and Ben out of the house, I had the place

to myself and the whole day ahead of me. I started by emptying out the food cupboards. First, old tins were lined up along the top of the work surface, as I checked each and every label for its 'use by' date. I was disgusted when I found a few were out of date. I shook my head dramatically.

*Someone could've been poisoned!*

Slowly, I weeded out every old tin, spice and jam jar and threw the lot in the bin. Then I took out a bottle of bleach and a scourer and scrubbed the lot. I wiped all the tins and scoured the bottom of the cupboards until they were germ free. Soon, everything was gleaming; it made me feel good to know I'd made a real difference. I placed the newer tins back, arranging them into different food groups. Beans sat alongside soup tins and away from tinned puddings. I wiped each one and lined them up in a neat row according to their height. Everything had a place and now everything was in the right order. I worked methodically; turning them around so all the labels faced forwards.

*Much better,* the voice congratulated me.

The spices had been scattered, so I arranged those that were still in date inside a neat box which I stowed inside a cupboard. The spices had looked messy before but now that they were hidden away, everything looked more streamlined. Once I'd done the cupboards and work surfaces I turned my attention to the furniture. As I took in my surroundings, my heart sank. The toaster was in the wrong place and the microwave well, that simply had to be moved. Everything looked wrong!

*How can they live like this?*

It was exhausting work but, by the end of the day, I'd managed to move and bleach everything which wasn't screwed down. I also binned anything which looked as though it'd seen better days. The kitchen table was a real struggle so I used my old tricks of the trade. Wedging my back up against it, I placed one foot against the wall and pushed and pulled until it was standing in the right spot. I finished off by bleaching and scrubbing both the walls and tiles with a scourer. By the end of the day I was absolutely knackered. I'd been cleaning non-stop for almost 12 hours but as I stood back and admired my work I felt exhilarated.

*Everyone will be delighted, especially Rob's mum!*

I glanced up at the kitchen clock. Rob would be home soon and I couldn't wait to see his face. Half an hour later, I was waiting by the backdoor when he walked in.

'Ta dah!' I said, spanning my hands out towards the kitchen.

Rob's mouth fell open with shock when he saw what I'd done.

'Err...' he stammered, trying to find the right words.

His face looked pale as though the blood had drained from it.

'Well, what do you think?' I asked.

But Rob didn't speak; he was taking it all in.

'Err yeah, it's good. It's... err... it's really nice,' he finally mustered.

'Do you think she'll be pleased then, when she comes back off holiday?'

Rob didn't answer; he was still busy doing a 360-degree turn in a middle of the kitchen.

'I've sorted out everything,' I said excitedly, opening up a cupboard, giving him a guided tour.

'See, I've put all the tins in here, and all the jars are in this one, over here.' I explained. 'It just makes everything so much easier to find.'

But Rob was still standing there with his mouth agog.

*I wish he'd say something, anything,* I thought bitterly.

'And I've had to throw a few things away. Not much,' I said noting the horror on Rob's face, 'I'm sure your mum won't mind because they were out of date anyway so, you wouldn't want to eat them.'

But he remained deathly quiet; I took it as a bad sign and shrugged my shoulders.

'You don't like it, do you?'

He looked at me and back at the kitchen.

'Yeah, I do,' he said in a small voice. 'And I'll tell you what: Mum's going to be really pleased when she sees it.'

'Do you think so?' I said running over to give him a hug.

'Absolutely. You've done a great job, Hayley.'

I was so happy; I couldn't wipe the smile off my face. Rob loved it and Kay would too. She'd be really pleased and then we'd become good friends. It felt nice to spend the rest of the fortnight in a clutter free kitchen. Before now, I'd hidden from Kay. I'd only ever ventured into the kitchen to grab a piece of toast because until now, it had never felt clean enough to me. But now it did, and I knew that Kay would be delighted. Everything was perfect, ready for her return.

The night before his parents flew home I gave the kitchen one last wipe down. I'd kept it spick and span. I smiled as I tried to imagine Kay's face when she saw it. But, as it turned out, Kay wasn't delighted. She was absolutely livid. Her suitcase had no sooner touched the floor then she was back in there, sorting it all out, putting things back to how they used to be. I was mortified and took it as a personal attack against me.

'But I thought she'd be pleased!' I complained to Rob.

He shook his head. I could tell he was embarrassed, playing piggy in the middle between the two main women in his life.

'It's her house Hayley, and she just doesn't want you touching her stuff, that's all,' he tried to reason.

I refused to listen because to me, it felt ungrateful and mean.

'This is about me. I thought she'd be pleased but I don't even get a thank you! I spent hours moving her stuff around and this is what she does. Well, good luck to her,' I huffed, folding my arms across my chest.

I was in a temper but it wasn't Rob's fault; it wasn't even Kay's, it was mine. But I was so wrapped up in my obsession with germs that I didn't realise just how bad I'd become.

COMING
CLEAN
LIVING WITH OCD

**CHAPTER 11**

# MORNING SICKNESS AND BLEACH

MY LEVELS OF hygiene were so impossibly high that if others didn't fall in line with them then I'd accuse them of being filthy.

One day, Rob moaned about me tidying up his bedroom. I was upset because I felt he should be grateful for my efforts and not complain about them.

'Do you have to do that right now?' he muttered as I sorted through a pile of papers.

'But it's all so messy!'

'No, it's not, it's fine.'

Only it wasn't, not in my book.

'It's you,' I snapped, 'You're abnormal. You're dirty because you've not been brought up properly!'

It was a horrible thing to say but part of me meant it because I didn't understand how people could live with such a mess. Rob seemed hurt, which made me feel guilty, but he didn't know about my compulsions or the voice inside my head which urged me to do these things. He was always immaculate in his appearance but it wasn't enough because I *needed* his bedroom to be the same. I wanted it to look like a showroom and having extra time on my hands didn't help one bit.

Thankfully, shortly afterwards, I managed to land a job at Boots Opticians working as an optical assistant. It wasn't my dream career because I knew I'd find it difficult working with the public. But I took it all the same because the job had a few perks, namely 40 per cent off makeup. It sounds shallow but my fear of germs meant I found my new job particularly challenging because some of the customers were just so gross. The majority were fine but the odd one smelt of urine, or had glasses caked in dead skin. The thought of their skin flaking onto my hands made me even worse and every opportunity I got I'd scrub between my fingers obsessively.

*I've got to get their germs off me!* I panicked as I stood at the sink.

Part of my job involved asking customers to rest their chin against a machine so that I could press a button which sent a small puff of air against their eyeball. I hated looking into people's eyes at such close range. All that skin and fluid made me feel queasy, especially when the eyeball was magnified through the machine. The closeness of customers left me cold. Sometimes my face would be so close that I could smell their breath and body odour – it made me want to retch. To be honest, I shouldn't have taken the job because I hated everything about it. During my lunch breaks I'd try and cheer myself up by visiting the makeup counters. I loved browsing through and testing out all the new products. It gave me a break from the shop but there would always be a dirty pair of glasses waiting for me when I returned. I wrongly thought I'd be in my element cleaning things but I hated it because it wasn't my dirt, and the fact that no one was ever as clean as me turned my stomach.

'How's the job going?' Rob asked later when he picked me up from work.

'It's okay, I guess.'

Although my colleagues were friendly, I never felt as though I fitted in. I was young and lacked confidence but I also secretly battled with intrusive thoughts. If one of my work colleagues looked over at me oddly, or answered me a little too sharply, then I became convinced they didn't like me. If I saw a few of them chatting or laughing away in a corner, I told myself they were talking about me.

*They think I'm a slapper,* the voice said. *They all hate me here because they think I look like a slag.*

They probably didn't, but that's how I felt. That's what the thoughts told me and slowly I started to believe it. My compulsions were coupled with this constant paranoia. I fretted that they thought I was a fat, common south Londoner, who wasn't as upmarket as they were. Feeling sad and alone, I asked for a transfer and went to work at Boots Redhill store in Surrey. I'd only been there for a few months when Rob and I decided to try for a baby but sadly, nothing happened. I was so disheartened that I confided in a relative. This particular woman already had two children of her own but she told me how lovely it'd be to have a new addition to the family.

'The best thing is that your baby will be the only one born right now so you won't have competition against another child,' she insisted.

I thought it was an odd thing to say but I was delighted at

the thought of our child being pride of place. However, the following day the same relative knocked at my front door.

'Is Hayley in?' she asked Rob, 'I've got something to tell you both!'

I was in the bathroom but I heard her voice and went through to greet her. I'd only just turned the corner but she couldn't contain her excitement any longer.

'Guess what? I'm pregnant! So there'll be two babies in the family!"

I felt as if she'd punched me in the stomach. She'd sat with me the whole afternoon and not said a word. She'd listened to me pour my heart out about trying for a baby but, less than 24 hours later; she'd turned up on my doorstep announcing her own pregnancy. I tried to force a smile but inside I was dying.

'Why didn't she tell me yesterday?' I cried after she'd left. 'Why did she let me go on and on, saying how wonderful it'd be to have a new baby in the family, the only one, when all the time she knew she was pregnant too?'

Most people would have just shrugged it off. Maybe she didn't want to burst my bubble but she had, and in spectacular style. Without warning, the voice was there again, mocking me.

*She did that on purpose and she came to tell me today, in front of Rob, because she knows I can't get pregnant.*

I still can't explain why she did it but her actions made me feel worthless.

We continued to try for a child and, six months later, I started to feel very peculiar indeed. I felt constantly nauseous. In fact, it got to the point where I couldn't move without throwing up.

'Urgh! What are you wearing, what's that aftershave you've got on?' I asked Rob.

'It's what I always wear, why? Don't you like it?'

'It's not that, it's just so strong. It makes me want to be...'

But before I could finish my sentence I fled to the toilet and threw up.

'Hayley, are you okay?' he said, popping his head around the door.

'I will be but only if you take off that bloody horrible aftershave!'

Soon, I was being sick all the time. It got so bad that I was throwing up dozens of times a day and it left me feeling worn out. Anything set me off, even my favourite Coco Chanel perfume.

'Rob, I think I might be pregnant.'

'Maybe it's just a stomach bug?'

But I was certain it was something more, so I did a pregnancy test. As soon as I walked back towards the bedroom, two blue lines appeared.

'I'm pregnant!' I whooped, rushing in.

Rob was totally gobsmacked but delighted. All those months trying, all those months I'd convinced myself I'd never get pregnant and now here we had a child of our own on the way.

'I think I better do another test, just to be sure,' I decided.

Rob nipped out to buy another pregnancy test kit, but even two more positive results weren't enough. It was only after the fifth test that actually I started to believe it.

'We need to tell Mum,' Rob said, his eyes flashing with excitement.

As soon as we told her, Kay leapt out of her seat and ran over to give us both a hug.

'That's brilliant news!'

Although Kay and I had never seen eye to eye, I could tell she was genuinely thrilled.

But the morning sickness soon took its toll. I'd only been at the new store for six months when the doctor signed me off work permanently.

'I don't know why they call it morning sickness,' I moaned. 'The only time I'm not sick is when I'm asleep in bed at night.'

It was true, anything would set me off. One day, Kay was cooking spaghetti bolognese downstairs in the kitchen. But the smell of mince mixed with the strong aroma of onions and garlic flipped my stomach. I was hiding away in Rob's bedroom but the reek of cooking drifted up the stairs and underneath the door. The mince stench had all but enveloped me as my mouth filled with saliva but I wasn't hungry, far from it.

'I think I'm gonna be...' I didn't even get the last word out. Instead, I ran with my hand over my mouth, straight for the loo to be sick.

Afterwards, every time Kay cooked, my mouth would fill up with saliva and tip me over the edge.

'What about eating ginger?' a friend suggested. 'I've heard ginger biscuits are supposed to be really good for morning sickness.'

I tried but I vomited them up as well. Nothing seemed to work. It was horrible because I was convinced that I smelled of sick. In a bid to combat it and the germs, I upped my washing and teeth brushing to another level. I brushed my teeth for so long and so hard it made my gums bleed. But I couldn't brush them over the sink because that's where the spit had been so I'd have a shower, climb out, wrap a towel around myself and then switch the temperature to cold. Then

I'd stand there with my head half inside the shower, brushing my teeth beneath the freezing cold water. It was the only way I ever felt clean enough. But soon, even that wasn't enough so I started to chew gum obsessively. Like a petulant teenager with extra attitude, I chewed and chewed until the minty freshness took away the stench of vomit. Of course, I didn't even smell but my mind convinced me otherwise. However, all the chewing gave me was an aching jaw. Eventually, the nausea subsided so Rob booked us a holiday in Portugal. We stayed in a self-catering apartment which suited me fine because it meant I wouldn't have to eat any meals out. One night he cooked us a lovely meal but as we settled down he looked around for the bread basket.

'We've more than enough here,' I insisted, but Rob was adamant and brought the basket to the table.

'Here,' he said offering me a sliced piece of baguette, 'take that bottom piece.'

I reached in but as soon as I removed it, I spotted a small square ring box hidden underneath.

'Go on then, open it,' He grinned.

'Oh my God!' I exclaimed. 'Is this what I think it is?'

'Take a look and see.'

As soon as I opened it and saw the diamond engagement ring inside my heart pounded, but this time, with pure, exhilarated joy. I started to laugh because Rob had fooled me with the meal and the bread basket – I hadn't suspected a thing.

'Oh, Rob,' I gasped, clasping a hand against my chest. I could hardly believe it was happening to me.

'Hayley,' he began his voice low and serious, 'will you marry me?'

I looked at him and back at the ring.

'Of course I will,' I said leaning forward to give him a kiss.

I'd never felt so happy in my whole life. Rob was the man I wanted to spend the rest for my life with, I'd known it ever since I'd climbed into his bloody mini! The rest of our holiday was blissful and, as soon as we landed, we couldn't wait to share the good news. As the icing on the cake, we discovered at my routine 20 week scan that I was expecting a boy. Rob was thrilled. However, being signed off work gave me even more time to indulge in my compulsion to tidy. Each day, I'd sit in Rob's bedroom hiding away from Kay and the outside world. The sickness had subsided but every time I was ill, I'd think about my head being stuck inside an 'unclean' toilet bowl. It made me retch until that became a vicious cycle.

'We need to get a place of our own,' I insisted.

I instinctively rubbed my hands against my pregnant belly as I spoke.

'It's the baby,' I told Rob, 'We need more room. We can't stay here.'

It was true, his bedroom was large enough for us but too cramped for a baby. Besides, Kay had been asking what our plans were because there wouldn't be enough room for the three of us. I didn't tell Rob the real reason I didn't want to stay – that I thought his house wasn't clean enough to bring a baby up in. I didn't even tell him that I constantly worried Snoop would attack and smother our child as soon as my back was turned. I didn't tell him any of these things because I didn't want him to think I was mad.

'I just can't stay here,' I said, beginning to weep.

I wept because inside I had a real fear something terrible would happen to our child. I convinced myself that our baby would catch a terrible illness or breathe in germs from the cat and get sick. At least if we had our own place I'd be able to control everything. I'd keep it clean all the time. I talked of nothing else until eventually, Rob buckled and we found a little rented house in Horley.

I'd already started taking driving lessons but the impending birth put even more pressure on me to pass. In fact, I *needed* to pass before the baby was born.

'It doesn't matter if you don't because you can always re-take your test,' Kay tried to reason.

Rob agreed with her but I wouldn't listen – I *had* to pass my test because I *couldn't* have a baby and not be able to drive.

*What if the baby gets sick? I'll have to get him to hospital. If I can't drive then we'll have to catch the bus. If we catch the bus, then my baby might get sick from one of the other passengers and die, and then it'll all be my fault!*

I knew my fears were irrational but with raging hormones and a growing baby bump, I was slowly going into mummy meltdown. So, when I passed my driving theory exam I was elated.

'I can do this,' I told Rob.

But when I failed my driving test on parallel parking, I was absolutely distraught.

'You can just re-take it,' Rob soothed, but I refused to listen.

'You don't understand I needed to pass my test, for the baby!'

I was almost eight months pregnant and we'd just got the keys to our new place but I felt totally isolated. At first Horley had seemed the perfect choice because it was close enough for Rob's work. But it was also ten miles from my friends and family and, with no driving licence, I knew I'd never see them. Rob urged me to put in for my test again and thankfully there was a cancellation and I was able to take it again just a few weeks later. By now I was heavily pregnant and I think the examiner was a bit dubious getting into a car with such an emotional woman! I took my test in Croydon – an area I knew well. On the actual day, the whole area was completely gridlocked so, although we inched along, I didn't really get much chance to show off my driving skills. It was a good job because I was still crap at parallel parking. With very little time for manoeuvres and faced with a hormonal new mum, I think the examiner took pity and passed me anyway. I was thrilled because at least now I had an escape from my self-imposed prison. But actually getting out of the house was much harder than I thought because my confidence was lacking. One day, I took a deep breath and started up the car engine. It felt odd driving on my own, without Rob or my instructor, but I knew I had to do it. I couldn't sit in the house on my own a moment longer because when I did, I cleaned. Mum was out at work but I drove over to her house and sat with Nanny Linda. We spent all day chatting and drinking cups of tea, because coffee made me ill. I'd had such a lovely time that I vowed to pop over and see her again but the next time I went to leave it felt as though my feet were glued to the floor.

*What if I drive the car and have an accident? What if someone crashes into the back of me and kills my baby? It'll be my fault because I'm so selfish. The baby will be dead and it'll be my fault.*

My hands were clammy and I stopped dead in my tracks. The imagined car crash scene played vividly inside my mind. I turned away from the door and slammed the car keys back down on the side.

*I couldn't risk it.*

Instead I took off my coat, pulled on some rubber gloves

and began to scrub the sink. From that moment on, I filled my days with cleaning. I bleached every surface and scrubbed both the floor and walls with a scourer. Sometimes I scrubbed the walls so hard that the paint came off.

It was 2004, and our son was due in less than a month. I told myself the cleaning was natural – it was just me 'nesting' because the baby was on his way. I was so convinced that I told Rob.

'This baby's due any day now,' I said. I was on my hands and knees scrubbing a kitchen cupboard.

'How do you know?' He asked.

'Because I'm nesting! That's what happens just before we give birth, we start to nest!'

It all seemed so harmless in the beginning but the rituals of obsessive cleaning had already gripped me. I scoured the bathroom in particular because of germs. I *needed* every surface to be as clean as possible. Our maisonette was modern inside with laminate flooring and bright, clean walls but still I scrubbed. The property had its own entrance. I was grateful because the thought of having to share a communal hallway filled me with horror. At least in our own space I was just cleaning *our* dirt. There was a communal garden but we didn't use it because we were on the first floor and had our own steps and decking area, which I cleaned too. Rob got up for work at around 6am, so I'd get up with him and shower. After he'd left for a day in the office, I'd start cleaning. Only my hours were longer than Rob's and often I'd still be cleaning when he returned home 13 hours later. He didn't think to stop or question me because he didn't know I'd been doing it all day, and I chose not to tell him. He realised I was a clean freak so he presumed every time he saw me with a scourer in my hand that I was just getting ready for the baby. My day would start with myself when I'd shower and wash obsessively from my toes upwards. Once dry and dressed, I'd make a start on the house. I'd empty the kitchen cupboards, cleaning every single tin. Then I'd scrub inside the cupboards just to make sure there were no germs lurking. I'd bleach the floor but I wouldn't use a mop because I was convinced it wouldn't get it clean enough. Instead, I got down on my hands and knees with a sponge and rationally sectioned off the floor, concentrating on one patch at a time. Thankfully, the floor was laminate so it was easy to clean. I'd scrub each section twice until I was certain I'd covered every square inch. There were five rooms in total and I'd spend the whole day working through them all on my hands and knees. The following day, I'd repeat the process all over again – it was never ending. Despite being heavily pregnant, I moved furniture. It didn't matter if it was large or heavy, if it needed to be moved then it was. The laminate flooring meant it would slide along nicely, without too much effort. Soon I was shifting the double bed, the TV unit, even the sofa on my own. Strangely, although I was doing all these things to protect my unborn child, it didn't occur to me that the stress and strain I was putting on my body could trigger an early labour. One night, Rob returned home from work to find I'd switched the sofa around.

'Why have you moved it?' he asked. 'Why do you think it looks better over there rather than here?'

I didn't have an answer because I couldn't explain it.

'Listen, I'm not happy about you moving stuff on your own because you could hurt yourself. You've got to stop doing it. Do you understand?' Rob insisted.

I knew he was right but the intrusive thoughts were so strong that I couldn't ignore them.

*If I don't move the sofa, then something bad will happen to the baby.*

However, the following day I shifted the sofa back to its original position.

'You're right,' I told Rob as soon as he walked inside the door. 'I've put it back because it looks better over there.'

Rob scratched his head. He didn't know what to do with me.

With only weeks to go, I insisted that we needed to buy some baby outfits so Rob drove us to Bluewater shopping centre.

'Let's grab something to eat while we're here,' he suggested.

My heart plummeted because I knew I couldn't eat there, not in front of strangers.

But Rob was hungry so we walked into a restaurant and sat down at a table.

'What do you want to eat?' He asked as his eyes scoured the menu.

'Hmm?' I replied.

I was busy looking around wondering how on earth I was going to manage to eat without anyone seeing me.

'Hayley, I said, what do you want to eat?'

'Oh, just a burger and chips.'

The food wasn't important; it was eating it, that was the tricky bit. By the time it arrived I felt sick to my stomach. I was all churned up and glanced around to see who was watching me. No one was but now I couldn't bring myself to eat because the fear was still there.

'Aren't you hungry?' Rob asked. He sounded a little disappointed – this was supposed to be a treat after all.

'Yeah, of course!' I lied, picking the greasy burger up in my hands.

My eyes darted around the table looking for a napkin. I

placed it on my lap, ready to hide what I'd 'eaten'. As soon as I took a bite I felt my throat close up and, try as I might, I just couldn't swallow. I waited until Rob had looked away, picked up the napkin and spat the meat into it. I continued this way until it looked as though I'd eaten something. I had, but it was in a soggy mush, hidden between the folds of the tissue.

'I can't eat any more,' I said placing the remaining half eaten burger back on the plate.

I glanced around again because I wanted to catch them out – I was so paranoid others were watching me. Without warning, an overwhelming sense of panic swamped me.

*I've got to leave here – now!*

'Rob,' I gasped, my breathing was fast and shallow. 'I need to leave; I need to get out of here.'

Rob looked at his food, he'd not finished but I couldn't wait – I had to leave NOW! He watched in disbelief as I jumped to my feet.

'I'm sorry Rob, it's just that... err... I don't feel well. I've got to get out!' I gasped as I headed for the door.

Rob looked up at me and back at his food – he thought I'd lost the plot! The waitress spotted us and came dashing over because she thought we were trying to do a runner without paying!

'I'm ever so sorry,' Rob told her, 'but we've had a family emergency and we've got to leave. Here,' he said pushing some notes into her hands, 'this should cover everything we owe.'

'Sorry about that,' I said a little later. I knew I'd overreacted and now I was going to have to try to explain why. 'I just felt really sick; I don't know what came over me.'

Rob wrapped a protective arm around my shoulder.

'It doesn't matter Hayley; all I care about is you.'

I felt awful lying to him but I didn't know how else to explain it.

That day we bought more clothes than one baby could want or ever need – I couldn't resist all the gorgeous little outfits. However, back at home I didn't just fold them and put them away in a drawer, I washed and ironed them and then did it again just to be sure they were properly clean. My compulsion to wash, iron and fold the baby clothes took me over until soon I was washing them every day. Then it shifted to the point where I was checking them over and over. I'd pull them out, put them in a pile, check, fold, and then re-fold. The ritual was relentless. With Rob at work, I spent the whole day tidying, re-organising and hanging washing out. Sometimes, the urge to check the baby clothes would overwhelm me even when Rob was in the house. I'd take them out but I was clever and always I covered my tracks.

'Aww, look,' I said one evening lifting up a babygro from the top of the pile, 'isn't this one cute Rob?'

He smiled and nodded over, but I did it with the next one, and the one after that.

'Yes, they're all lovely, Hayley,' Rob sighed.

I could see his eyes glazing over because it was boring; I was boring, but he didn't realise I was performing a ritual: I was checking the baby clothes. Rob just presumed I was excited about the birth. I was, but the need to check and re-check the clothes time and time again was so compulsive that I couldn't help myself. I had to make sure they were clean enough for our baby because he'd be so fragile and pure. Rob wanted this child as much as I did but he didn't want to spend his entire evening looking through baby clothes!

'Oops,' I said pretending to knock over the pile so it was a mess on the floor. 'Oh, I'll just have to wash and fold these again before I put them back in the drawer.'

It was a lie. I didn't *have* to wash or fold them, I *needed* to. It was a calming ritual and one I'd perform again and again. The following morning I unpacked some cot sheets and held them up against the light to check. Then I sniffed them.

*Hmm, they definitely didn't smell right. They were a little musty; I needed to wash them.*

So I did. I washed them even though I'd washed and ironed them all the day before. I washed them until my hands dried out and my skin peeled and cracked. In my head I knew it was madness but I couldn't stop myself because, if I stopped, then the ritual chain would be broken, and if the chain was broken then maybe something bad would happen to our baby. Soon, there weren't even any maybes about it. If I didn't wash, iron and fold the clothes and the sheets then something *would* happen. I was certain of it. Everything had to be perfect because our baby would be perfect, pure and untainted, and I couldn't let anything or anyone contaminate him.

## CHAPTER 12

# *GERMS ON THE MATERNITY WARD*

WE WERE STANDING inside Woolworths when I felt a sudden twinge. I clutched my bump protectively.

'Are you all right?' Rob asked.

I was close to my due date but I'd been the one who'd insisted we go shopping to buy even more stuff for the baby.

'Yeah, I'm fine,' I lied through gritted teeth.

I reached over and picked up an antique looking baby sign.

'Oh, look at this. It's gorgeous. Shall we...' I began to say but, before I could get the rest of the sentence out, I doubled up with pain.

The agonising throb ripped through my body like a bolt of electricity as my stomach tensed and hardened.

'Hayley?' Rob called.

But I couldn't reply because another vicious pain stabbed through me, almost forcing me to my knees. I grabbed at Rob's hand to stop myself from falling. I was holding the sign in my other hand but the pain was so intense that I started to cry.

'Hayley, what's the matter? Is it the baby?'

The other shoppers turned, it made me feel worse. I looked up at Rob and shook my head.

'No, nothing's wrong with the baby, I just think I'm going to be sick.'

I didn't want Rob to go into a blind panic because, if he knew I was in labour, he'd call someone over and then I'd have everyone fussing around me.

'Just get me to the car,' I gasped as I clutched my stomach.

Rob helped me along and held open the shop door. As I waddled outside I felt all eyes on me. I'd really wanted to buy the sign because it said 'Little Prince's Room'. But the pain was so bad that I'd thrown it back on the side. The little prince, it seemed, was already on his way.

'Something's not right,' I wept as soon as I sat down the passenger seat of the car.

'What do you mean?' Rob gasped in a state of panic.

'It is the baby, Rob. I think I'm in labour!'

The blood drained from his face.

'The baby! Are you sure?'

'Yes, no... I don't know.'

The problem was it was our first child and I really didn't know if I was in labour or not, but it certainly felt like it. Rob wasn't sure what to do so he pulled out his mobile phone and called his mum. I noticed his hands were trembling as he punched in Kay's number.

'Yes, that's right... she's got pains,' he said relaying the information to her. 'They're in the front and in the... back?' he asked, turning to face me.

I nodded as I huffed and puffed at the side of him. Not surprisingly, Kay told him to take me straight to hospital.

'Right!' he said dropping the phone.

As the car engine fired into life I remembered I'd left something behind.

'Rob, my bag! If we're going to the hospital then I need to go home and collect my bag.'

Rob was in a state, all he wanted to do was get me to the hospital as quickly as possible, but I was adamant.

'I need it! It's got all my things inside,' I argued, making him turn the car around.

The car tyres screeched as Rob did a three-point turn in the middle of the road and we headed home.

'I'll get it,' he said jumping out as soon as we'd pulled up outside but I refused to sit and wait.

'Hayley, what on earth are you doing? We have to get you to hospital!' Rob gasped when he saw me climb out of the car.

'I just need to get a few more things from inside,' I replied, waddling up the steps to the front door.

Poor Rob, he was absolutely panic-stricken, but his stress levels reached fever pitch when he saw me nip into the bedroom and turn on my hair straighteners.

'Christ, what on earth are you doing now?'

I ignored him and calmly lowered myself down in front of the mirror. I picked up the straighteners and smoothed them through my hair.

'Hayley!'

'Rob, I'm doing my hair!' I snapped.

My labour pains were still coming and going at regular intervals but, right now, my hair seemed more important.

'Your hair? Can't it wait?' Rob said exasperated.

He was fidgety – his nerves totally jangling. Every time I flinched he went into a panic because he thought he was going to have to deliver his son on the bedroom floor!

'For God's sake, leave your bloody hair! It doesn't matter!'

Although the pains were stabbing both in the front and back, I knew I wouldn't be able to leave the house until my hair and makeup were absolutely perfect.

'I want to look okay for when the baby arrives.'

Rob looked at me as if I was completely nuts, and not for the first time. But how could I tell him or explain?

*I can't go to hospital without my hair and makeup done; if I did then everyone will judge me and think I'm a bad mother.*

It was madness of course but to me, it made perfect sense at the time. I even spent a few extra minutes glueing on a pair of false eyelashes.

'Hayley, we haven't got time for this!' Rob insisted.

But I knew what he was really thinking.

*At this rate, I'm going to have to deliver the bloody baby if she doesn't hurry up!*

A short while later, fully glammed up, I climbed back into the car.

'You can take photos of the baby but not me,' I reminded him for the umpteenth time as I tried to concentrate on my breathing. 'No photos of me, understand?' I insisted, my eyes wide and serious. 'Although I know someone's going to come in and try and be bloody David Bailey!'

I winced as another crushing contraction ricocheted through my body. By the time we reached East Surrey Hospital, I was taken to the maternity suite where I was examined by a midwife. Disappointingly, I was only one centimetre dilated.

'You're kidding me?' I huffed as she delivered the bad news. 'All that pain for a single centimetre?'

I still had another nine to go and wondered how I'd survive it all. I'd wanted the labour to be over and done with as quickly as possible but the medical staff sent me home. Looking back, it's hardly surprising given the fact I'd turned up with my hair straightened and my nails and makeup fully done. I hardly looked like a woman about to give birth!

'You need to go home and get into a hot bath; it'll lessen the pain,' the midwife advised me.

'But we don't have a bath. We live in a maisonette and we've only got a shower!'

We weren't sure what to do until Rob came up with a plan. He put me in the car and drove over to Kay's house. She looked a little shocked when she saw me waddling up the path.

'We need to borrow your bath, Hayley's in labour!' Rob gasped as soon as we'd stepped in through the door.

I wanted to protest but the pain was excruciating and I didn't have the strength to argue. I climbed the stairs but as soon as we reached the bathroom door, I reeled back with horror because I remembered the bathroom and how 'dirty' it was.

'I'm not getting in that until you clean it,' I said pointing towards the bath like a complete diva. I couldn't help it; my obsession with cleanliness wouldn't allow me to dip even a toe in before it'd been fully bleached.

Rob knew better than to try and argue with a hormonal clean freak in labour so he got to work on his hands and knees, scrubbing the bath both inside and out.

'Don't forget to use the bleach!' I called as I tried to concentrate on my breathing.

A few minutes later, Rob popped his head around the bedroom door.

'All done!'

But as soon as I walked inside the bathroom I decided the rest of it needed to be cleaned too.

'You need to bleach it all, including the floor!'

Rob shook his head in despair.

'Bleach the floor because I don't want to catch a verruca!' I said insanely.

He knew I'd completely lost it but did exactly as I'd asked just to shut me up. He even unrolled a brand new bathmat and lit some candles to help soften my mood. Finally, as I lowered my stomach down into the warm water it began to soothe me.

'Better?' Rob asked rubbing my back.

'Yes, thanks.' I sighed and I meant it, every single word, because I knew he'd have moved heaven and earth for me.

In the end, my moment of calm only lasted another 30 minutes because soon the pain was so intense that I started 'mooing' in the bath, like a cow!

'Hayley, are you alright?' Rob asked, a little frightened.

'Do I look alright?' I snapped. I didn't mean to but by now I couldn't help myself.

I started to wail: 'It's no good; you've got to get me back there. You've got to go back to the hospital!'

There was a loud knock on the door. It was Kay.

'Rob, can I have a word please?' she said, beckoning him outside.

He left the bathroom door slightly ajar so I could hear every word.

'That poor girl needs to go to hospital and you need to get her there NOW!'

I was grateful to Kay because I couldn't have spent a moment longer in that bath.

As soon as I arrived, a midwife checked me over for a second time. I was devastated when she told me I still had a long way to go. In fact, I was so upset that I burst into tears, again. In the end, Rob took me home because we only lived five minutes away. Without a bath available, Rob twisted on the shower and gently showered my back with warm water in an attempt to soothe me. I tried to ride the pain out but the shower didn't help one bit. The hospital midwife insisted I go home so that I could get some sleep, but it was impossible. The pain wouldn't let me rest. Rob rang them back but they told him to try and encourage me to eat. He ordered a pizza but I refused to touch it. A few hours later, at 4am, I was howling like a wounded animal when I staggered to the toilet and had a 'show'.

'Rob, you need to take me back because something is definitely happening!'

Rob was as exhausted as I was but somehow, we managed to climb into the car and drive back to the hospital.

'If I have to make this journey one more time...' I said, clasping a hand over my mouth.

The motion of the travelling car coupled with contractions was making me nauseous. By the time we reached the maternity ward I'd had enough and was effing and blinding like a trouper! Now I didn't care who saw or heard or me.

'Get this fucking baby out of me!' I wailed. I writhed in agony as the midwife helped me up onto a bed in the labour suite.

I was given some gas and air but soon it wasn't even touching the sides. I was squirming so much with the pain that they had to drag me from the bottom of the bed right up to the top again. At one point it became so bad that I thrust out a hand and grabbed Rob's shirt. I pulled so hard that I ripped the poppers clean off the front of it but he didn't dare complain. Instead he asked if I was okay. It was the wrong question to ask at that precise moment.

'No, I think I'm going to die!' I wailed dramatically.

'Shall I get your Mum?'

'No, just get me something for the pain!'

Rob buzzed the senior midwife who came to check on me.

'I don't think she'll be able to push now – she's too exhausted,' she told him, before turning her attentions to me. 'I think we'll give you an epidural. Hayley, is that okay?'

Okay? I could have kissed her! Even though I had a life-long pathological fear of needles they could have stuck a fork in my back as long as they gave me something to take away the pain. By the time the drugs kicked in, my head had stopped spinning on my shoulders and I was no longer a woman possessed.

'Better?' Rob asked.

'Much better,' I sighed.

I'd been in labour for almost 48 hours but now, drugged up to the eyeballs, for the first time I'd started to feel a little better. Once I'd calmed down I took in my surroundings. As I glanced around the room, I saw things I'd not noticed before. My eyes widened as they took in the walls – the paint had chipped off in patches and the floor looked grubby, like it needed a good scrub. The floor had a type of marble effect so it was hard to see were the patterns started and the dirt ended. It looked as though it'd been coated with tiny specs of dirt and blood. The more I looked, the more I saw – it was absolutely filthy!

*Oh my God, it's so dirty!* I panicked. *I'm going to have our baby in this dirty old room!*

My face was a mixture of horror and repulsion.

'When the baby's born, please don't let them put him in one of those hospital cribs.' I begged Rob, pointing towards a cradle behind him.

'But Hayley, they have to.'

My mind whirred with thoughts of bacteria and bugs.

'But what if it's dirty? What if the baby catches something?'

The voice inside my head went into overdrive.

*I wonder how many germs are in one of those plastic cribs. My baby is going to go into that, and then he'll get sick.*

'Don't worry,' Rob said trying to calm me down. He patted my knee, trying to reassure me. 'It's alright because they'll wrap a blanket around the baby before they put him in.'

He was only trying to help, but the thought of a dirty hospital blanket made me ten times worse!

'No they're not! They're not wrapping my baby in a hospital blanket! What if it's not clean?'

The palms of my hands began to sweat as I started to have a panic attack.

'Rob, we must have a blanket of our own they can use. We must give them a clean blanket!'

But moments later when full labour kicked in I soon forgot about the crib and the blanket. All I wanted was to give birth to a healthy baby boy.

I'd tried to touch up my makeup throughout the labour but the pain was so bad that I'd managed to sweat and cry most of it off so, in the end, I gave up. It was a slow process and two days after my labour had started in Woolworth's, our son Calum slowly arrived. The senior midwife was being aided by a student who was on hand to observe, learn and generally help out.

'Do you want the baby delivered onto you, Hayley?' she asked automatically.

I shook my head in horror.

'Eurgh no!' I gasped.

The young midwife seemed a little shocked and asked again as though I'd misunderstood her question, but my answer was the same. She looked at me and then at Rob.

'Are you sure, it's just that most mothers usually...'

I didn't let her finish her sentence.

'No, I do want him but please could you wipe all the blood off him first?'

Both nurses looked up as if I was completely bonkers!

'Well, if you're sure...' the older one said.

I could tell she didn't approve of my request. After all, what other young mum would say such a thing? But then other mums weren't like me. I was desperate to hold and nurse my son but as much as I wanted him, the thought of holding him covered with blood repulsed me.

*He'd be covered in dirt. Even though it's my blood, it'd smear against my skin and infect me with germs. If I was dirty then I might give him germs, then they'd multiply and spread. Christ, they could even kill him!*

I wanted to hold my baby but I needed him to be cleaned first because he'd come out all messy and I didn't want to see all the blood and gore which went along with childbirth.

'Baby will be here soon,' the student said chirpily as I heaved some more.

*Shut up!* The voice inside my head shouted back at her.

I worried how I'd cope because no one, not even Rob,

*Above*: My big sister Lauren and I sitting in the sunshine – with the dreaded fishpond behind us!

*Below left*: The love of my life Rob and I, all ready for Christmas celebrations.

*Below right*: Enjoying a lovely day at the beach with my two best boys.

*Left*: At my wedding with my dad. I couldn't stop panicking about the thought of falling over in front of everyone.

*Right*: Just married! And feeling very, very tired…

*Left*: It was a perfect wedding day and I was so happy to share it with everyone, including my lovely mum and stepdad.

*Left*: Even after the wedding, I still did not feel like I was skinny or brown enough.

*Below*: My handsome son Diezel and I looking happy, just after his dad and I were married.

*Above left*: Although I try my best to control it, my OCD does make me very anxious about my boys. I wasn't keen to let Calum go on this ride on his own!

*Above right*: Rob with our boys. Much to my delight Rob had finally acquired a tan.

*Below*: Enjoying a cosy moment at Center Parcs with my husband and my three amazing children. My favourite people in the whole world!

knew how I felt inside. I wanted to kiss and cuddle Calum – I wanted him close so that I could feel his skin against mine but I didn't want him to be dirty.

'Please clean him first. I need him to be nice and clean,' I said, repeating myself as I gave one last enormous push.

Rob knew I was a clean freak but even he looked shocked.

I waited for Calum to make a noise so I knew he was okay. His first cry was so loud and unexpected that it took both of us by surprise. This was real. Now we were parents. The midwife picked up him up in a bundle and cleaned and weighed him before handing him over to me. She placed him on my chest and, as soon as I saw him, all my fears melted away. Instead I felt an immediate rush of love. A short while later the student midwife asked if she could check him over. I looked on proudly as she picked him up but then she did something quite unexpected, she crooked her finger and placed the tip of it inside his mouth. As soon as Calum sensed it, he sucked at it greedily.

'Oh, I think he's hungry!' she grinned.

She was testing his sucking reflex but I wanted to punch her in the face because she'd just contaminated my baby.

*If I could move right now, I'd rip your head off!* The voice screamed inside my head. *Get your finger out of his mouth or I'll bloody chop it off!*

I wanted to scream and shout at her to leave my baby alone but I was worried I'd be labelled irrational or mad. The midwife hadn't been wearing rubber gloves and the thought of her sticking her bare, unsterilised finger into my baby's mouth made me want to gag.

*How do I know how clean your hands are?* I seethed to myself.

I held my arms out for Calum and she handed him back to me. Our bond was immediate but now she'd done that, I vowed never to let my baby out of my sight again.

*I can just imagine where your hands have been*, I thought bitterly as she tidied up and left us alone in the room.

'I didn't like her,' I said turning to Rob after she'd left. 'She shouldn't have put her finger inside his mouth – what was she thinking of?'

The thought of contamination stayed with me for the next hour so, as soon as we'd been discharged to the ward, I was determined to wash my son.

'He's only been wiped but I want to bath both him and myself,' I insisted.

'But we don't recommend that. It's best to just wipe your baby down with cotton wool. I'll go and fetch you some and a bowl of warm water,' the nurse said before turning to leave.

'No,' I gasped, grabbing her arm, 'you don't understand. I don't want to wipe him, I want to bath him. He's dirty and so am I!'

She shook her head and called over her colleague who backed her up. They both urged me not to bath Calum yet, but despite their protests I refused to back down.

'Look,' I said, my patience wearing thin. I was exhausted after such a long labour and I really didn't feel strong enough to argue. 'He's my baby and I want to bath him. I want him in a bath now!'

The two women looked at each other. I think they realised I wasn't going to give in. Maybe they presumed I was just an overprotective mother, I don't know. Whatever they thought, eventually they found me a shallow baby bath for Calum. I couldn't wait to get clean because I felt so dirty and polluted. Rob and I picked up Calum and the baby bath and walked into the hospital bathroom. To be honest, the nurses probably thought I was a complete pain in the arse but I couldn't explain to them why I needed to wash my son; I knew they'd never understand. Once I was clean, I immediately felt better. As soon as I returned to my bed I grabbed my bag and started to reapply my makeup. I think some of the other mums on the ward thought I was vain but I had to do it because I knew I'd be scrutinised by everyone – them, the nurses, the doctors, even the visitors.

I tried to breastfeed Calum because I wanted to lose my baby weight quickly even though the thought of doing something so natural secretly repulsed me. However, when he failed to latch on, I then beat myself up about it because I felt as though I'd failed.

'I'm a crap mother,' I wept to Rob.

'No, you're not. You're brilliant,' he said wrapping a reassuring arm around me.

But no matter how wonderful and supportive Rob was, I didn't listen because I truly believed I was a crap mum.

A short while later the nurse approached me to talk about breakfast.

'The other mums eat together in the breakfast room so they can chat and get to know one another,' she said breezily.

The thought of eating in front of strangers made me want to heave.

'No,' I insisted. 'I'm not hungry.'

'But you've got to eat something. You've got to keep your strength up, for the baby,' she said smiling down at Calum, who was gently dozing at the side of my bed.

I refused point blank so she dispatched a bossy health care worker who appeared suddenly at the foot of my bed.

'What shall I put you down as having for dinner then?' she said, holding a pen and a form in her hand.

'No, I'm fine. My husband's going to bring me in a sandwich.'

But she refused to take no for an answer.

'What if he doesn't? What if he forgets? I need to put you down for something?'

I watched the pen as it hovered above the paper waiting to tick a box.

'Okay, something plain then,' I sighed. I just wanted her to go away and leave me alone. 'I'll have chicken or something.'

I had no intention of eating hospital food because I didn't know what was in it or who'd cooked it. Besides, the ward felt too dirty to sit and eat in.

A few hours later, Mum, Nanny Linda and my three sisters burst into the ward desperate to see Calum.

'Oh he's gorgeous, Hayley,' Mum beamed as she picked him up out of his crib.

I didn't flinch when Mum held him or when Nanny Linda and my three sisters insisted on having a cuddle. It was weird. I didn't object to family members holding my son, I just didn't want strangers to do it. Rob saw his chance and nipped out to fetch me a chicken sandwich, which I ate later behind closed curtains. If I had to eat then I would but I couldn't eat a cooked meal, it had to be food I could pick at – picnic style food. As I ate, Rob turned to look at the hospital curtain drawn around my bed.

'I don't want to look at the other mums,' I said by way of explanation.

But the truth was I didn't want the others to look at me. After that, I kept my curtains closed all the time. The nurses didn't approve and a few wandered over to open them again.

'We need these open so we can keep an eye on you and your baby and make sure you're both okay,' one sniffed, eyeing me suspiciously.

'But I just want a bit of privacy; I want to keep the curtains closed.'

The nurse stopped pulling the drape and turned to face me.

'You won't get to know any of the other young mums with the curtain drawn, now, will you?'

I didn't care. I was in hospital out of necessity, not to make new friends. The nurse tried to reason with me but I refused to listen and, as soon as she'd gone, I pulled the drapes shut again. I liked it when they were closed because it kept the rest of the world out. It stopped all the watchful eyes from looking over at me, judging me. It also acted as a barrier because behind the curtain, Calum and I were trapped inside our own bubble where nothing could harm or pollute us.

Later that day, another nurse who'd just started her shift pulled the curtains to one side. The sudden noise of metal rings dragging against the track made me look up.

'We need you to keep these curtains open,' she insisted.

'I want to keep them shut, it's more private.'

'But we need to keep an eye on you and we can't if you're hiding behind these,' she said swishing the curtain back round.

Some of the other mothers looked up and it made me feel totally exposed. I hated the way they looked over at me because I was convinced they were judging me and my skills as a mother. Also, there were germs on the ward – other peoples' germs. I imagined coughs or sneezes as droplets floating through thin air and landing inside Calum's cot. With the curtain open we had no protection but the nurse was adamant.

'I hate it here Rob, I just want to get home,' I wept.

I was exhausted and all the strength had drained from me until I barely had the confidence to fight back. Rob realised and went over to speak to the staff.

'If Hayley wants to keep her curtains drawn then you have to let her. She wants a bit of privacy, that's all,' I heard him say at the nurses' station.

'But we like to keep the curtains open,' one of them replied.

Rob refused to back down and argued my case. In the end he won. After that, I got to keep the curtains shut all the time. It made me feel less anxious. I don't know what Rob thought of my strange behaviour. Maybe he presumed I had a bout of baby blues, who knows? Only I knew the truth: that this was something I couldn't control. I didn't want to get to know other women on the ward because I was worried they might contaminate Calum. Instead I begged Rob to get us discharged.

'Seriously, you've got to get us out of here. I can't stay another night.'

He tried his best, but they refused because I'd not been checked by a doctor and I was told I'd have to wait until one could be found. I didn't want to stay there another minute because my environment contained strangers and germs and I hated not being able to wash or clean when I liked. Even as I sat in my hospital bed I worried.

*What if someone's died in this bed? What if they had something horrible? What if I catch it and give it to Calum?*

I prayed a doctor would come along soon. Thankfully, a few hours later she did and, because I'd had no complications, she agreed I could be discharged that same afternoon. As I packed up my things I glanced down at the speckled grey floor. The edges of it looked dusty and dirty in corners where the mop hadn't quite reached. I looked closely at a speck on the floor and thought how much it looked like a tiny splatter of dried blood. Bile rose inside my throat and I clamped a hand over my mouth to stop myself from being sick. I couldn't wait to get out of my bed and this filthy pit of a hospital. I couldn't wait to take my precious baby to a place of safety where everything was clean and all the surfaces had been bleached. Only there would I finally be able to relax because, only there, would I have control. Nowhere else ever came up to scratch when it came to being clean – nowhere.

As soon as I walked through the door at home, I felt able to breathe again. I started to relax because I was surrounded by familiar and clean things. Two hours later, Rob's mum and dad came to visit Calum. They'd wanted to come to the hospital but I didn't want to stay longer than I had to. As we sat chatting, I watched from a distance as Rob's mum crooked her finger and did exactly the same as the trainee midwife. Calum automatically sucked against it, causing palpitations inside my chest.

*Oh my God, she's been stroking that cat and now she's put her finger inside Calum's mouth!*

My mind whirred with panic but I couldn't reason with my irrational thoughts as they danced around inside my head.

*Now he's going to get sick. Now he's swallowed germs and he'll get sick and die!*

Suddenly, I decided I didn't want anyone else to touch or even hold Calum. He was my boy and I only wanted Rob or me to comfort him. Earlier that day I'd been fine when my family had held him but now I wasn't because everything felt wrong and out of control. I stood up, walked out of the living room and wandered into the bedroom. I closed the door behind me, lay down on the bed and cried my eyes out. Moments later, Rob appeared as a shadowy figure in the doorway.

'Are you okay Hayley?' he asked, his voice full of concern.

'Please can you get the baby back off your mum?' I begged. 'She's just put her finger in his mouth.'

'Did she? Oh, Hayley, I'm so sorry babe.' Rob said as he turned and headed back to the front room.

He didn't tell his mum what I was upset about instead, he was diplomatic and explained I was shattered after the long labour.

Tucked away from everyone else, I walked over towards the bedroom window and drew the curtains. I felt totally exhausted and flopped onto the bed where I rested my head against the soft, fresh pillow. It'd been a hugely emotional day.

A short while later, I heard Kay's voice call to me through the bedroom door.

'Bye Hayley,' she whispered gently.

'Bye,' I replied as I buried my face deep into my pillow and sobbed.

Kay hadn't done anything wrong so why did I feel so bad? I hated feeling this way but the saddest thing was I didn't know how to make it stop or go away.

COMING CLEAN
LIVING WITH OCD

# CHAPTER 13

# *STERILE WORLD*

THE FOLLOWING MORNING there was a knock at the door. It was the health visitor. She'd called to check on me and Calum. Rob showed her in before disappearing off into the kitchen to make a cup of tea. I was on the sofa with my baby boy nestling gently in my arms. After a polite bit of chit-chat, the health visitor looked up at me, a little concerned.

'And how are you feeling Hayley?' she asked.

I tried my best to put on a brave face. The truth was, after spending 48 hours in labour I was truly knackered but, as most new mums do, I didn't want her to think I wasn't coping, so I lied.

'Oh, I'm fine,' I said managing a smile.

'Are you sure? Are you okay... it's just that you look really pale.'

PALE. The word hit me like a right hook to the side of my face. It felt like taking a bullet straight to my heart.

'Do I?' I asked, a little perturbed.

I hadn't been near a sun bed for ages but I'd religiously slathered on fake tan. But pale? The health visitor didn't realise I had an obsession with being brown. Nor was she to know only a few years earlier I'd spent every spare hour lying on sun beds in a bid to achieve the ultimate tan. It sounds ridiculous but in my mind, the health visitor calling me pale was just the same as her calling me fat. Her remarks wounded me but somehow I managed to keep it all inside. However, after she'd left I thought of nothing else.

*If she thought I was pale then she must think I'm fat. She was actually trying to say that I looked fat,* the voice repeated inside my head.

I didn't say anything to Rob but he noticed I was quiet and wanted to know why.

'It's nothing,' I lied. 'I just didn't like her very much. She was so rude. In fact, I think I'm going to put in a complaint against her.'

Rob looked aghast but I was determined not to let her make me feel bad.

*I'll prove her wrong,* I vowed, *I'll show her how tanned I can be!*

But the stark reality was I was worried about seeing the health visitor again.

*The one who'd called me pale and fat, the one who thought I was useless.*

She hadn't said those words but that's what she thought, she thought I was a useless mother.

Later that night, I inspected my body in front of the mirror. It had been swollen and stretched by childbirth but underneath I was still the same old Hayley. However, the more I looked the more I realised she was right. I did look pale: pale for me. It took me ages to get off but when I eventually did, I fell into a fitful night's sleep. My dreams were full of people criticising me, people coming to take Calum off me because I was a useless and unfit mother. In the early hours of the morning, when Calum awoke, I stood by his swinging cradle. All I'd ever wanted was a family of my own but so far I'd failed miserably. I couldn't even breastfeed my baby. Calum wouldn't be getting the best from me but it also meant I'd carry around the extra baby weight for longer, perhaps forever. I cursed myself and wandered into the kitchen to fetch him a bottle. Calum nuzzled blissfully against my shoulder. I loved the smell of him, the purity of his skin against mine. I felt an overwhelming urge to protect him. I was his mum and I couldn't let anything or anyone harm him. This was my job now. As I stood rocking him to and fro I glanced over at the rinsed baby bottles neatly lined up on the side. They'd been sterilised using Milton fluid. The bleach smell immediately made me feel better and brought me comfort because bleach meant they were clean. Bleach meant every single bug or speck of bacteria had been eradicated. Bleach was good because bleach kept my baby safe. The following morning, I grabbed hold of the Milton sterilising fluid and used it to bleach everything in sight. Nothing was left untouched. Everything was scrubbed and cleansed within an inch of its life. Satisfied there was nothing left behind, later that morning I calmly picked up the phone and called Rob at work.

'Could you hire me a sun bed?'

'Hayley, are you sure, do you think that's...' Rob began but I cut him off mid-sentence.

'Just get me a sun bed Rob, I can't cope with looking pale and fat any longer,' I said, beginning to weep.

Deep down I think Rob knew it was crazy but he organised one to be delivered to the house. As soon as it arrived I immediately felt my anxiety lift. This was my answer.

*The health visitor won't be able to call me pale or fat anymore, not after I've used this. I'll show her.*

Smothering myself in tingle cream, I checked on Calum. He was safely asleep tucked up in his car seat. I positioned the seat far enough away from the sun bed but it was still within arm's reach so, if he woke up, I'd be able to rock him to sleep again.

*Nothing will stop me from getting on that sun bed. Nothing.*

I switched it on and lay down. As soon as the halogen glow began to sear at my skin I felt better, as if a blanket of calm had washed over me. I basked in the glow, allowing the harsh light to burn my skin, eradicating every last pale pigment. Just as the bleach had washed bacteria from the floor and work surfaces, so the sun bed would wipe away the poisonous paleness and turn it a deep golden brown.

'You seem happier,' Rob commented as he walked in through the door later that evening.

'I feel it,' I said wrapping my arms around his neck and planting a kiss on the side of his face.

'Thank you for hiring me the sun bed. I just feel so much healthier.'

Overnight that one sun bed had totally transformed my life. Rob was just relieved to get the old Hayley back because when I was tanning, I was happy. It was as if slowly, with every day that passed, I was returning to him, piece by piece. But thirty minutes wasn't enough and, with no one there to watch me, I'd twist the timer until soon I was spending every spare minute of every day on it.

'Will you watch Calum? I'm just going on the sun bed,' I asked Rob later that night after we'd had tea.

Not that I'd eaten much because now I was on a new mission – to get slim and tanned.

'Didn't you get chance to go on it today?' Rob remarked as he rocked Calum in his arms.

'No, he was grizzly all day, that's why he's so tired now.'

It was a lie. I was spending all day on the sun bed because the health visitor was coming back at the end of the week and I wanted to prove her wrong. If I looked tanned, slim and in control then she wouldn't think I was useless, fat and pale. I'd make her eat her words. The compulsion to tan my skin continued until my next follow-up appointment and, when she finally knocked on the door I was ready and waiting for her.

'Hi, come in,' I said breezily.

She smiled as she walked in through the front door but as she did, she turned to do a double take.

'Wow, you're really brown. Have you been away?' she asked, unzipping her coat.

'No!' I laughed. 'Come on through, Calum's just in here.'

I showed her through to the front room where Calum was fast asleep in his car seat. I automatically lowered myself down and sat beside it so that I could gently rock him.

'So,' she said, 'What's your secret?'

I shook my head; I didn't have a clue what she meant.

'Your lovely tan! How come you're so brown, surely it's not been that sunny here?'

'Oh no,' I said trying to explain. 'I've got a sun bed so I've been using that.'

The health visitor sat back in her chair.

'And where do you put Calum when you're using the sun bed?'

I bristled slightly, now she was looking for something else to find fault with.

*She was trying to make out I wasn't looking after my baby.*

'Oh no, he's beside me in his car seat,' I explained. 'I just use it when he's asleep.'

'Right,' she said, although it was clear she didn't approve. 'But you don't put Calum near it, do you? He's only a baby...'

'No, it's fine.' I replied. I was relieved because I knew I could answer this question. 'I just keep him at arm's length so that I can rock him if he wakes up'.

The health visitor reeled back in her chair with a horrified look on her face.

'But you understand that sun beds are dangerous, Hayley, don't you?'

The tone in her voice immediately put me straight on the defensive.

'You mustn't let Calum get too close to it because he's only a baby.'

I nodded my head but inside I wanted to die. I couldn't win. I was either a fat, pale mother or I was a heartless bitch, putting my baby at risk. It was the worst thing she could say to me because so far I'd spent every waking hour making sure no harm came to Calum. I'd scrub the floor and kitchen work surfaces daily just to make sure he didn't get sick and now this silly woman was criticising me for using a sun bed! After she left I was in pieces so I called Rob.

'I hate that woman,' I sobbed. 'She's horrible. I never want to see her again!'

'Why,' Rob asked. 'What's she said?'

'She pretty much labelled me a bad mother and I am; I'm a crap mother! I hate her Rob. She's got something against me.'

Of course Rob was furious and rang the doctor's surgery to put in an official complaint. He told them in no uncertain terms that the health visitor was never to call at our house again.

'What did they say?' I asked him later.

'Don't worry, you won't have to deal with her again.'

I was relieved, relieved that I'd never have to see the awful meddling woman again – relieved that I'd be able to continue getting browner and browner. Soon I was spending so long on the sun bed that I was falling asleep on it for hours at a time. I didn't worry about skin cancer or the harmful effects it could have on me, all I cared about was looking 'perfect'. But that perfection soon extended to my environment and before long I was cleaning the house from top to bottom every day. If I wasn't on the sun bed, then I'd be bleaching everything down. Calum's baby bottles were my main priority. I'd bleach them more than once just to make sure they were totally clean. Then I'd wash my hands again and again because I was worried they weren't clean enough and I'd infect my baby. Eventually, with the constant rituals of sun bed, cleaning and bleaching, the skin on my hands dried and cracked but I still couldn't stop. Now I was caught on a sick merry-go-round and I couldn't get off. The rituals and compulsions to bleach, wipe and scour every surface exhausted me yet, no matter how shattered I was, I couldn't stop, because if I stopped then I was certain something bad would happen to Calum, and it'd all be my fault. Instead, I'd take out his freshly sterilised bottles, smell them, and clean them over and over again.

One afternoon, I was lying on the sun bed when Calum

became grouchy. He'd been asleep for a few hours but now all he wanted was a cuddle. His cries made me jump to my feet. I automatically went to him to pick him up and that's when it happened. I'd only just applied the tingle cream and I'd totally forgotten, but as soon as I moved my hands and spotted the red patches on his skin I was sick with worry.

'Oh my God!' I gasped, going into a blind panic.

The tingle cream had reacted against Calum's skin causing it to turn an angry red. The marks scared me because I knew it was my fault. I ran to the sink and washed the cream from my hands and arms before picking him up again. Frantic with worry, I ran a baby bath so that I could wash him. Dipping my elbow into the water, my eyes filled with tears. The red marks had subsided a little but even though it'd been a total accident, it didn't stop the guilt and self-loathing I now felt.

*The health visitor was right, I am a crap mother*, the voice in my head screamed.

The water immediately soothed Calum who settled down within minutes and although the red marks had already started to fade, I washed him three more times just to be certain I'd got all the lotion off. Afterwards, I cursed myself.

*What were you thinking?* I asked.

*I did that to him. I'd made him uncomfortable.*

Of course I knew it was ridiculous. I knew the red marks had just been an immediate reaction through direct contact with the lotion. I knew my baby was okay, but for weeks afterwards I was wracked with guilt. I convinced myself I was a bad person and an even worse mother. It got so bad that I begged Rob not to go into work because I didn't want to be alone with my baby in case I did something else.

'Please stay; please don't leave us here alone,' I wept.

At first Rob made up excuses but eventually he had to return to work because he was needed there and we needed the money. As he closed the door I sat helpless, a heap of tears in a corner of the room. With Rob at work I tried to keep myself busy. I spent all day going from one ritual to another. I'd bleach everything down, unstack, clean, and then re-stack the kitchen cupboards one by one. Then I'd get down on my hands and knees and scrub every inch of the floor. The need to clean was relentless.

One weekend, when Calum was just a few weeks old, I asked Rob if we could visit Redhill, because I wanted to buy some baby toys.

'Let's look in here,' I said pointing towards a large department store.

We wandered around for a bit picking up various soft cuddly toys and that's when I spotted her out of the corner of my eye: a middle aged woman with grey hair. She was standing there staring at Calum.

'Come on,' I told Rob, 'let's go and look around the other side.'

We walked into the next aisle but moments later she was there again, looking inside his pram. She smiled at Calum and then up at me but I didn't smile back. Instead, my body went into full panic mode.

*She's going to steal my baby,* the voice warned. *Watch her, don't let her take Calum!*

'Here,' I said pushing the buggy over to Rob, 'Can you take him for a bit?'

I wanted Rob to push the buggy because he was stronger and, unlike me, I knew he'd be able to fight her off if she tried to snatch the buggy. We carried on but I couldn't concentrate because every aisle we walked down the lady was there. It was as though she was following us, watching and waiting.

*She was waiting to steal Calum!*

I picked up a toy, popped it back and then watched as she picked up the same toy.

*She's definitely following us,* I told myself.

I thought back to my days working in Boots; there'd been a man who often came in to have his glasses checked and cleaned. I'd felt a little bit sorry for him at the time because every week he'd pop into the store and tell us he'd won the lottery.

'I'll take you all out for dinner,' he insisted.

Of course he never did because his 'win' was all inside his head. One of the other girls told me he was a patient at a mental health unit not far from the town centre and now, looking at the woman, I wondered if perhaps she was the same.

*Maybe she's crazy and she's going to take Calum from me?*

Soon I'd convinced myself she was going to steal my baby. The thought whirred inside my head the more she followed until finally it all became too much. I couldn't take my eyes off her as every sinew in my body told me to run.

'She's going to steal him, Rob. That woman is going to steal our baby!' I blurted out.

Rob looked over at me and then at the woman who turned away.

*She's guilty, that's why she'd turned away. She knows I've rumbled her – that I know what she plans to do.*

'Come on,' I said grabbing Rob's arm. 'We've got to go!'

Rob looked at me as though I was crazy.

'Come on, hurry up! I want to leave; I want to go home NOW!'

The woman seemed to hover and then, without warning, passed us by. As her steps speeded up so did my heartbeat.

*There's definitely something not right about her. She looks mad; she looks like the type of woman who'd steal a baby.* The voice convinced me.

I watched the woman like a hawk as we left the shop. I even checked behind me to make sure she wasn't following us. Soon we were back in the car and we'd left the strange woman far behind but the intrusive thoughts were still there, rattling around inside my brain.

Not long afterwards, I had a routine appointment at the doctor's but after the incident with the woman, the thought of leaving the house petrified me. I knew I'd have to venture out in the car yet every muscle in my body pulled me back inside, telling me not to go.

*What if someone crashes into the back of us and kills Calum?*

Despite my fears, after hours of psyching myself up, I finally loaded up the car with Calum and his buggy.

'There you go, sweetheart,' I said, clipping him into his baby seat.

I took a deep breath of air. I felt proud that I'd managed to get past the front door, never mind into the car, but now it was time for the difficult bit. I felt nervous and edgy throughout the journey. I constantly checked the rear view mirror to make sure no one was getting too close behind us. Eventually, I pulled up outside the surgery and unloaded Calum's buggy. His pram had cost an absolute fortune and had been a present from Rob's mum and dad. I'd asked for it because I knew it was top of the range – the best one on the market. I carefully unclipped Calum and gently laid him inside. A short while later, after seeing the doctor I left the surgery and went back to the car. I clipped Calum into his baby car seat but, try as I might, I just couldn't collapse the buggy. I pressed various buttons but it was as though everything had jammed. The more I struggled, the more rigid and stuck it became. It wasn't long before Calum got bored and started to cry. In a complete fluster I picked up the phone. I called Rob at work to ask him what to do.

'Just release the trigger, the one on the side.'

But that was the problem, I'd already pressed it and nothing had happened.

'It's not working, Rob,' I panicked.

By now it had started to drizzle with rain and Calum's screams had reached fever pitch. He was so loud that patients coming out of the doctor's surgery looked over to see what the commotion was about.

'Try it again,' Rob said calmly.

'Rob, I'm doing it but it won't fucking work!' I said, losing my patience.

The more people looked, the worse I felt and I began to weep.

'Hayley, calm down,' Rob soothed.

'Rob, it won't fucking work!' I screamed.

It wasn't his fault but now I was taking it out on him.

'Listen,' he snapped back, 'what do you want me to do about it? I'm at work!'

I tried the trigger again but the pushchair was completely jammed and refused to budge. A lady spotted me and wandered over to see if she could help.

'Is everything alright?' she asked gently.

Her concern made me feel worse as I flushed with embarrassment.

*What sort of crap mum can't even collapse her own baby's pram?* The voice taunted me.

'It's the trigger thing on the side,' I told her pointing down at it, 'I've been pushing it, but it won't collapse,' I explained as Rob listened in through the phone.

'Tell her to push it down,' he said, butting in.

'Rob, it's not working. It's stuck!'

The lady tried her best but she couldn't manage it either. In the end, her husband, who'd been sat waiting in his car, got out to see if he could help.

'Here,' he told her, 'let me have a go.'

By now I was scarlet red. Calum was screaming at the top of his lungs, it was slashing down with rain and every single person had turned to watch us.

'Shush darling,' I said, trying to soothe Calum as the man struggled with the pram.

'It's not working,' I said, giving Rob a running commentary.

I cursed myself.

*Why did I have to choose the flashiest pram in the shop? Where had it got me? Piss wet through with a screaming baby, that's where!*

In the end, even the man admitted defeat.

'Sorry, it just doesn't seem to want to go down,' he sighed.

I was absolutely mortified as more people stopped to watch the unfolding non-folding buggy show.

'Rob, what am I going to do?'

'Just shove it in the bloody boot, Hayley.'

'But you don't understand! It won't go in!' I sobbed.

Even though the man and woman were still standing there I didn't care. Right now I felt like the most useless mother on earth. I was crying because I was both embarrassed and angry.

In the end, we managed to take the top carriage off and shove it into the back seat. The wheels and rest of the chassis stood up in the back of the boot but at least we'd got it all in.

'Thank you,' I told the couple as I jumped into the driver's seat to make a quick exit.

I couldn't drive away fast enough. As the car engine revved into life I waved them a cheery goodbye and wiped away my tears of humiliation with the back of my sleeve. We'd spent a good 40 minutes trying to get the bloody thing to collapse but it hadn't. Calum was crying because he was due a feed and I hadn't brought one with me because we were only supposed to be ten minutes. The truth was I'd just wanted the ground to swallow me whole. I'd always hated others looking but now I felt the man, woman, even the whole street was judging me.

*What will they think of me now? I know what they'll think – they'll think I'm a crap mother, and I am!*

As soon as we got home I fed Calum and then I called Rob.

'I bet that couple go home and talk about me. I bet they laugh about what a crap mum I am,' I sobbed.

'But you're not! Listen, it's only a bloody pram Hayley! Don't let it get to you.'

But that was the problem; it *had* got to me and now I couldn't think of anything else.

*I bet they tell their friends over dinner parties about the useless mum who didn't know how to collapse her baby's pram. I'll be a laughing stock. I deserve to be laughed at and talked about because I am useless.*

The voice was right, I was a crap mum and I felt it and, at that moment, I never ever wanted to leave the house again.

## CHAPTER 14

# *THE DOUBTING DISEASE*

'I'VE HAD A good month this month so let's treat ourselves. Let's go to Bluewater shopping centre,' Rob suggested, early one morning.

He'd noticed that I'd become more withdrawn from the world.

'Err, I'm not sure.'

'Oh come on. You, me and Calum, it'll do us good. We could buy some nice things for him, what do you say?' Rob asked, raising his eyebrows.

I was sitting on the sofa cuddling Calum. I hadn't been out of the house for weeks following the buggy incident. It was as though the humiliation had stolen away my confidence. Of course, Rob knew all about it because I'd gone over it all in minute detail but secretly, I think he thought I was overreacting.

'Of course they won't think you're a bad mother. I bet the

same thing happens to a different mum every day. It's just a stupid, trendy buggy,' he'd said laughing the whole incident off.

But to me, the nightmare with the buggy had just proved to the rest of the world what a crap mother I was. It'd unmasked me and all my failings.

'So, do you want to go to Bluewater?' Rob asked again, breaking my thoughts.

'Okay, but I'm not driving,' I insisted.

'No problem. Here, give me Calum, and go and get yourself ready,' he said, holding out his arms to take the baby.

It was still early but he knew it'd take me ages so he was giving me plenty of notice. As I applied my makeup I thought about the trip ahead. I didn't mind being in the outside world but only if Rob was with me. I knew I'd be able to cope because he'd be on hand to help me with the unpredictable buggy or screaming baby. All I really knew right now was I couldn't make a trip like this alone. By the time we arrived, Bluewater was bustling with shoppers. It was a busy Saturday and there were lots of families enjoying a day out. As Rob and I mingled in the crowd, for the first time in ages I started to feel normal again. We were just like every other young family. I had a beautiful baby and a loving partner – I realised what a truly lucky woman I was. All I had to do was stop beating myself up about every little thing.

Rob bought lots of things including clothes for Calum. It'd been a good day but as we walked around from shop to shop, Calum started to get hungry.

'We need to feed him,' I decided but I didn't want to sit down in a restaurant because I'd have to order a meal and I didn't want to eat in public. 'I'm not hungry,' I told Rob, as a quick as a flash.

Thankfully, he wasn't hungry either so I told him to hand Calum to me so I could feed him in my arms. Although he was hungry, Calum seemed to take forever to finish his bottle and soon my arm had gone completely dead so I handed him back to Rob. I smiled as he gently cradled him in his arms and watched as Calum's tiny mouth clamped the teat of the bottle and began to suck. Eventually, he drained the entire bottle.

'That's my boy!' Rob said, grinning down at him.

He winded Calum but when he tried to put him back down in the buggy, Calum cried, so he picked him up again.

'Hey, what's the matter?' Rob said pulling a face.

As soon as he'd picked him up, Calum stopped crying so he walked along with the baby resting against his shoulder. By this time we'd reached the first floor. There was a clear glass barrier in place which meant you could look through it onto the floor below but it was high enough to stop shoppers from toppling over the edge. Without warning, I looked back at Rob with Calum on his shoulder and a random thought passed through my mind.

*We're really high up and you're going to throw our baby over the top of the barrier, I just know it.*

My body went into panic as, frame by frame, I pictured Calum sailing through the air and landing on the hard marble floor below. I could actually see it inside my head – Rob throwing Calum over the edge of the barrier.

*Then he'll crash onto the ground below,* I thought grimly.

I shook my head to rid myself of the thought but all I could see was a vision of Calum's limp and lifeless body. Try as I might, I couldn't shake it out of my mind until I convinced myself that Rob was actually going to do it.

*You're going to kill my baby!* The voice screamed loudly.

Panic flooded through my veins and my breathing became erratic and shallow. I was so stricken with fear that I actually thought I was going to have a heart attack. I couldn't look at Rob because I was terrified he'd do it right there and then.

'Hayley, are you okay?' he asked, bringing me back into the moment.

'I'm fine.'

Only I wasn't. The voice repeated it again in my mind and my heart was thumping inside my chest.

*It's just a mad thought; Rob wouldn't really throw Calum over the edge,* I reasoned.

I tried to rationalise the thought but the more I told myself I was being ridiculous, the more vividly I pictured Calum falling through the air. I imagined myself stretching out to try and catch him, but missing. The more I thought it, the more plausible it seemed.

*What if Rob didn't mean to throw Calum over the edge? What if he slipped and tripped or what if someone bumped into him and knocked Calum from his arms? It'd kill him and I wouldn't be able to save him.*

The grim vision repeated itself like a sick horror film. I tried to focus ahead and not look at Rob or the vast drop below. I hoped the horrible thought would go away but it didn't and now it was stuck, playing again and again, like a broken record. Deep down, I knew Rob would never harm our baby and I felt guilty even thinking it. I wanted to ask Rob to hand Calum over to me, maybe then I'd feel better? I was just about to ask when another thought stopped me in my tracks.

*What if Rob hands Calum to me and I have a moment of madness? What if I go crazy and drop him over the edge? What if I stumble and Calum falls over and smashes to the ground below. What then? I'll have killed him. I will have killed my own child!*

My hands were trembling but my mind was frozen with fear. Rob was a brilliant dad – I knew he'd never do such a wicked thing, but what about me?

*Would I do it? Of course not, but what if I did? What if I did something so terrible that even Rob couldn't forgive me?*

I knew I was being irrational but at the same time I worried because there was always an outside chance it might happen. I couldn't tell Rob what I was thinking because he'd think I was mad or, even worse, he'd think I was actually capable of such a terrible thing. He'd think I was crazy! But the random thoughts refused to budge. Instead they made me doubt everything. I'd doubted myself as a mother, I'd doubted myself as a person, Christ, I'd even doubted Rob! But the harder I tried not to think about it the more I did until it had taken me over.

'Please put him back inside the buggy,' I begged.

Rob looked puzzled.

'Why? He's fine.'

'No, I don't like it; please put him back in his pram!'

*If I don't take my child off my husband now, get him back inside the buggy and leave now, then something bad will happen to Calum and it'll all be my fault,* the voice warned.

It was plaguing me, like a big bully inside my head. Only this was one bully I couldn't escape from because it was there with me every minute of every day. The fear that Calum would die was so real I could almost taste it. The bully inside my head was blackmailing me. If I didn't do as it said then my baby would die. I had no choice; I had to give in to it because I couldn't bear to think of the alternative.

Rob tutted. He didn't have a clue what was wrong but he did as I asked. As soon as Calum was safely strapped back in his pram the anxiety lessened.

*At least if he's in his buggy you can't throw him over,* I thought. *At least he's safe and I won't accidently throw him over the edge either.*

I knew the thoughts were crazy but by now I couldn't help myself or make them go away. In fact, as we walked towards the exit, the grimmer they became. As Rob pushed the buggy onto a downward escalator my mind went into overdrive.

'Careful,' I said grabbing the side of the buggy with my hands.

I watched in a heightened state as each metal step folded in on itself in at the bottom. I saw how sharp the serrated edges were as they dipped and folded before disappearing into the mouth of the escalator.

*What if Calum's buggy falls down and he topples out?*

I shook the thought from my head – this was madness. It was torture, but try as I might, I couldn't stop the terror vision from seeping in until I pictured it as clearly it as if it'd just happened before my eyes – baby Calum lying at the bottom of the escalator with his head embedded in a metal step.

'Please be careful, please make sure the buggy doesn't fall,' I begged Rob as we glided to the floor below.

'It's fine, Hayley, don't panic,' he said tightening his grip on the buggy's handle. 'Calum's okay, I've got hold of him.'

In some ways Calum being strapped in made it worse because I visualised the whole thing falling over and collapsing in front of us. I pictured blood oozing from Calum's scalp as his life ebbed away. Without warning, my palms began to sweat until they were almost dripping with fear.

'I don't like it in here,' I said, turning to face Rob. 'Can we go home now?'

Rob didn't have a clue what was wrong with me and I couldn't explain either, but thankfully he agreed to leave. As we headed back to the car I breathed a sigh of relief because outside in the fresh air everything felt so much better. Outside was good because inside there were strangers and potential death traps. As I breathed in the cold damp air, a car passed by us. It'd been travelling slowly but I worried just how close it'd been.

*What if it suddenly went out of control and smashed into us, killing Rob and Calum, what would I do then? How would I cope?*

I closed my eyes for a moment and tried to banish the image of a mangled pram and two bodies out of my head.

'Are you okay?' Rob asked.

I opened my eyes.

'Yeah, I'm fine. I'm just tired, that's all.'

But I wasn't fine. I was far from it. I was still trembling when I climbed into the car. All I could think about was getting home and shutting the door on the rest of the world. As soon as I'd fastened Calum into his car seat I felt better because I knew he was safe from harm. But the moment Rob turned the key in the ignition my mind wandered as I pictured the journey ahead.

*What if someone crashes into us on the way home? What if...?*

'You okay?' Rob asked again. 'It's just you're really quiet.'

And I was. I was quiet because the voice and all the intrusive thoughts were screaming inside my head, swamping my mind in blackness. I couldn't even begin to explain or understand it but it was exhausting and totally consuming. I turned to look out of the window as the world passed by in a blur. I wiped away a solitary tear. I longed to be 'normal', to be able to walk along the street with my baby without fearing the worst. Rob didn't notice I was crying because I was good at hiding my fears from him and everyone else. These were my personal demons and I'd just learned to live with them.

COMING
CLEAN
LIVING WITH OCD

## CHAPTER 15

# *NEAT BLEACH*

NOT LONG AFTER the disastrous Bluewater shopping trip my cousin announced she was getting married. Normally, I would have been delighted and I was, but the thought of finding something suitable to wear sent me into a blind panic.

'I need to find something!' I panicked later that evening although I knew another shopping trip would be torturous.

I still felt fat after giving birth and although the weight was coming off, it wasn't coming off quickly enough. Rob drove me into town to have a look but I couldn't find a thing to wear so, reluctantly, we travelled back to Bluewater. I tried not to think about the balcony or the risk of Calum falling over the edge. Instead I beat myself up in each and every single shop. I was horrible, ugly and fat and nothing fitted me. As I wandered from one store to the next I hated myself even more because all I could see was a big, fat, Hayley staring back at me in the mirror. I told myself it wasn't really me – it was the mirror in the shop. Maybe they were designed like that so that they'd show up every lump and bump? But it didn't make me feel better as I struggled with one dress after another. I couldn't even fasten some which left me even more disheartened. Then I thought of who'd been in them before.

*Who's already tried this dress on?* I wondered. *What if they had B.O. or some horrible skin disease?*

I quickly unzipped the dress and threw it straight to the floor. I couldn't get it off fast enough.

'Alright in here?' the assistant asked, pulling the curtain slightly to one side. I wanted to scream at her to leave me alone. But instead I quietly nodded my head.

'Well, if you need a different size, just let me know,' she smiled.

I wanted to smack her in the face. How could I ask for a bigger size from her? She looked so pretty – she looked so perfect.

*I bet if I asked her for a bigger size she'd go and tell the others in the shop. She'd tell them what a fat bitch I am.*

I angrily pulled on my clothes. I pictured the changing room assistant outside making faces behind my back, bitching and gossiping about me with other girls on the shop floor. It was so real that I could almost hear her.

*'I don't know why she's trying that on – she's far too fat for it and she looks a total mess.'*

Of course, the assistant wasn't really saying any of these things and when I finally emerged from the changing room, she simply asked if I was keeping the dress.

'No,' I replied without looking as I brushed straight past her and over to Rob.

'What was it like?' he said as soon as he saw me.

'Don't ask. It looked horrible. Come on, let's try somewhere else.'

We looked in various shops but if I wasn't worried about Calum, I was worried about going into the changing rooms. If I wasn't fretting about that then I wondered who'd tried on the same clothes before me. I even worried about putting my feet on the floor in case I caught a verruca. My mind was exhausted!

'It's no good,' I told Rob. 'I'm too fat, I can't find anything!'

But he refused to give up and drove me to Brighton, to see if I could find anything suitable there. I couldn't. In fact, the more dresses and outfits I tried on, the more my confidence drained from me like grains of sand in an hourglass. It was hopeless. In the end, I went to the wedding wearing something I'd had for years because it was the only thing that still fitted me. It didn't stop me feeling shit about myself: if anything, it made me feel ten times worse. From that moment on, I vowed to shop online. At least then I didn't have to try on any 'dirty' clothes. At least then I knew they'd always arrive freshly packaged and neatly folded. It made me less anxious knowing I was the only person who'd ever tried the garment on. Yet despite this, the intrusive thoughts refused go away. They manifested themselves inside my head and, when I wasn't cleaning I was worrying about what might or could happen.

'Do you fancy a night out?' Rob asked a few weeks later.

'What about Calum?' I fretted.

'It's not a problem; I've asked Mum and she said she'd love to babysit.'

Kay kindly babysat for us but I still couldn't relax

because by now, Kay had two dogs and I was certain they'd rip him apart.

Around this time, Rob realised I was fussy about where I ate so he'd managed to book us a table at Pizza Express – it was the only place I felt safe. We'd been before and, at first, I'd panicked but when the waitress allowed me to choose my own table, I felt better. That's when I'd spotted it, right at the back, with a chair facing in towards the wall. It was perfect because I was able to face the wall while Rob faced the other diners. Soon it became the only place I'd eat at. It was hardly a cure but at least it was progress. That evening Rob had reserved the same table and it was waiting for us as soon as we arrived. We'd not been there long when I began to panic. I thought of Kay's dogs and worried about Calum being in the same house.

*What if they attack him or rip him apart? There've been lots of dog attacks in the paper and on TV recently. If it could happen to other people then why not to us?*

I looked at Rob.

'Text your mum, check if Calum's okay?'

Rob sent a short text and moments later his phone beeped on the table with Kay's reply.

'What does it say?'

'It says Calum's fine – everything's fine,' Rob said, twisting the phone around so I could read it for myself.

Despite Kay's text, I couldn't stop thinking about the dogs. It got so bad that, within the hour, I begged Rob to take us back so we could pick up our son.

'You two are early,' Kay said. She seemed a little surprised when we walked through the door.

Rob looked at her and shrugged as if the whole night had

been a complete waste of time. I didn't care what he thought because right now Calum was safe and back in my arms. Afterwards, I was reluctant to leave him again because I convinced myself that no one could look after Calum as well as I could. No one. However, the sad reality was that although Calum was my main priority, cleaning our maisonette had become my focus because if I didn't clean it from top to bottom every single day then he would get sick and die.

*If our baby died then Rob would hate me because it would all be my fault.*

I became so obsessed with germs that I was pouring neat bleach on everything, including my hands. The chlorine burned against my flesh but I liked the stinging sensation because it reminded me that as long as it burnt my skin, it was burning away bacteria lurking between my fingers. Only when the burning sensation had reached fever pitch would I run to the sink and wash it off. The skin on my hands slowly dried and cracked, making it even more painful the next time I washed them but pain was good, because pain and bleach meant my hands were sterile. After that, I started to use neat bleach to wash my hands the way most people use soap. Part of me knew it was wrong but the other half couldn't stop. I had to do it so Calum didn't get sick.

Yet however much I moved the furniture around, I couldn't move the rooms or even knock down walls because we lived in rented accommodation.

'I hate this kitchen,' I complained to Rob one day.

He was eating his food at the table but he lifted his head as I spoke.

'Why, what's wrong with it?'

I couldn't put my finger on it because it was impossible to

try and explain. Besides, he'd never understand. The rooms were in the wrong order and no matter how much I shifted the furniture they always would be. We needed to move, it was the only way I could make everything right again. In the end something prompted our move faster than we'd planned. One day there was a knock at the door. I answered it to find our elderly landlord standing on the doorstep.

'Hi, I just thought I'd let you know that I'm not going to be around for a while because I'm going to visit relatives in America.'

'Lovely!' I said before wishing him a safe journey but, as soon as I shut the door, I had an overwhelming feeling of doom.

'He's not coming back,' I suddenly said to Rob. I couldn't explain it; I just had a really strong feeling it would be his last journey.

'What do you mean?'

'I dunno, I just don't think he's going to live that long.' The uneasy feeling swept over me but then Rob agreed.

'Do you know, I was just thinking exactly the same thing but I didn't like to say anything.'

We looked at one another and a cold shiver ran down my spine.

A month or so later there was another knock at the door, only this time it was the landlord's son.

'I've come to tell you my dad has died.'

My stomach lurched, I'd suspected as much. Even so, I told him how sorry we were but there was something else he wanted to ask.

'I wondered if you could make yourselves scarce on Wednesday next week?'

I asked him why.

'We're flying his body back from America but it's been a complete nightmare because they've insisted on it being sealed in a metal container,' he explained.

'So why do you need us out of the way, next week I mean?'

But I was quite unprepared for his bizarre answer.

'Because we want to bury him in the garden. It's what he would have wanted.'

'What?!' I gasped.

The son was adamant. The house belonged to him and his father's final wish was to be buried in his own garden. I nodded my head and closed the door in a state of shock. I turned to Rob.

'Surely he means they'll just scatter his ashes around?'

'Yeah,' said Rob. 'Of course, that's what he meant.'

Only it wasn't. Days later, I was awoken by the sound of a small digger reversing in the back garden. I pulled back the bedroom curtains and gasped when I saw it claw and dig a deep hole, large enough for a full-sized coffin. The following day was the day of the 'funeral' but I couldn't wait to leave. Rob had already left for work so I wrapped up Calum and drove over to Mum's to spend the day with Nanny Linda.

'A body! In the garden?' she shrieked. 'Surely not, they must mean his ashes?'

'Yeah, that's what we thought until yesterday when I saw them digging a great big bloody hole!'

I stayed with Nanny Linda until later that night, until I was sure Rob would be home. As soon as I closed the front door, I popped Calum down and went over to the window to look.

'Oh my God!' I gasped clasping a hand to my mouth. 'There's even a bloody tombstone with flowers around it!'

I don't know if they buried a dead body in the garden or

just scattered ashes but, after that, I couldn't wait to move. I couldn't wait to leave the old property because not only were the rooms in the wrong place, there were ashes, or possibly a body, in the back garden!

We moved to East Grinstead and four months later, when Calum was a year old, I discovered I was pregnant again with another boy. By now, my cleaning had gone into overdrive. One day I'd spent all day cleaning when Rob walked into the kitchen. As he did, his arm brushed against something, catching it and seconds later, a tin of thick white gloss paint was knocked onto the floor. The lid popped off and the sticky white mixture spilt out across the laminate floor. When I saw it, I lost the plot.

'What have you done?' I screamed like a demented banshee. 'I've only just cleaned that and now it's filthy!'

I was so furious that angry tears spilled from my eyes. I thought of all the hours I'd spent on my hands and knees scrubbing the floor. I'd bleached every square inch of it but now it was all for nothing, because now the paint had contaminated it and messed it up all over again.

'It was an accident, honest!' Rob said, holding his hands up in protest.

I glared at him.

*Why would you do something like that? Why on earth would you throw white paint all over the floor? Don't you think the floor is clean enough, is that it? Do you want me to get down on my hands and knees and scrub it all over again?*

The thought whirred around inside my brain stoking my anger. I shot Rob a hateful look.

'Jesus, I'm sorry, okay?' he said, trying to scrape some of the paint up onto the lid.

But instead of making it better, he made it even worse. It was enough to tip me over the edge and the fury which had been boiling up inside bubbled to the surface until I couldn't contain it any longer.

'You fucking wanker!' I screamed ripping the toaster from the wall and throwing it directly at his head.

Rob glanced up. He saw it coming and managed to duck just in time. The metal toaster sailed through the air, missing his head by inches and smashed into pieces against the opposite wall. Rob looked up at me in horror. He couldn't believe I'd just thrown a toaster at his head but then again, neither could I. But then Rob didn't know what it felt like to be me. All those hours cleaning had left me exhausted and frazzled. Even though I used rubber gloves, the neat bleach had left my fingers calloused, cracked and sore but now I'd have to clean it and them all over again – it was never ending.

'I can't believe you just did that,' Rob said finally straightening up.

He looked visibly shaken but so was I, only my body was trembling with rage. I didn't even know where it'd come from because it'd been so sudden and intense: I'd frightened myself. Now I was too angry to even look at him. Kneeling down, I started to try and mop up the gloss from the floor. The paint was as sticky as treacle but in many ways as liquid as water. It'd gone everywhere so Rob grabbed a cloth to try and help.

'Leave it!' I hissed. 'Just leave it; you'll only make it worse!'

Just like looking after Calum, I knew only I could clean it up properly. It had to be spotless because no one else could get it as clean as me. As Rob picked up the pieces of the shattered toaster I realised what I'd done.

*What if I'd killed him?*

'I'm sorry,' I said beginning to weep as remorse swept over me.

'Hey, it's okay, it's only a toaster,' Rob said taking me in his arms.

'But I shouldn't have thrown it. I could have really hurt you.'

'Yes, you could have but you didn't, and I'm fine.'

But I wasn't fine because my need to clean had all but consumed me. In fact, it'd taken over my life. Cleaning didn't even soothe me anymore; it just added to my stress. Now it'd become a big mountain I had to scale every single day. Later that evening, when Rob made a joke about the toaster I laughed. It made me feel better because I was glad he'd managed to see the funny side but then I worried because I knew it wasn't funny. The bleach and the cleaning had taken over my life and it'd become a vicious circle. The more I cleaned, the more I needed to – there was no end to it. The following day when I dragged myself out of bed, it was still there waiting to be cleaned and scoured all over again. To make matters worse, I was permanently knackered because my morning sickness was as bad as before. In fact it was so bad that I spent most of my pregnancy with my head down the toilet. The thought of all the germs in the loo set my senses on high alert and I wasn't happy until my lungs throbbed with the stench of neat bleach. At first the smell would overpower me and make my eyes water. The vapours would catch at the back of my throat and choke my breath away. I continued to live like this, caught up in a sick merry-go-round of bleach and scourers for the rest of my pregnancy. At eight months pregnant, we moved again because we needed two bedrooms, so we found a cottage in Dormansland.

A short while later, when my labour pains started I was

ready. I'd already insisted to the midwife that I wanted my second child be born at a different hospital.

'The last one was filthy, horrible and dirty,' I told her.

She tried to talk me round but I refused to listen.

'I'll go anywhere else, just not back there.'

In the end, she gave up and I was referred to a hospital in Sussex. Unlike last time, I decided that this birth would be perfect. Before I left, I sat in the bath and shaved my legs until they felt smooth and silky. Then I spent ages applying fake tan because I didn't want the nurses to think I wasn't up to the job.

*A good mother was someone who could look after herself,* I reasoned. *If you can't look after yourself then how on earth can you look after a baby?*

*No one would judge me and, if I looked my best, then they wouldn't.*

As I pulled the straighteners through my long dark hair, I checked my hospital bag one last time. Right at the top, in pride of place, was my new nightie. I'd bought it especially for the occasion. It was designer and had cost £90, but I didn't care because I thought it was a small price to pay for a 'perfect' birth. By the time we'd arrived at the hospital the labour pains were intense. However, the lift was out of order so I was forced to walk up three flights of stairs to the labour ward.

'Wow, don't you look glam?' the midwife remarked as soon as she saw me.

She typed my details into a computer and showed me to a bed. Shortly afterwards another midwife popped her head into the room.

'I just need to take some blood from you' she said breezily, and that's when I realised she was a final-year student midwife.

My heart plummeted. I remembered the last one and how

she'd stuck her finger in Calum's mouth. My body tensed as she plunged the needle into my skin and she detected my unease. It shook her confidence because soon she was struggling to get a single drop of blood out of me.

'Sorry, I'll just have another go,' she flustered, sticking in the needle again and again.

My arm looked and felt like a bloody pin cushion before she finally admitted defeat.

'I'm afraid I'm going to have to send you back down to the blood department to see if they have any more luck.'

'You're joking, right?' She wasn't.

With the lift out of order, I had to walk back down the three flights of stairs. I huffed and puffed and occasionally stopped as the contractions gripped me.

'Is another one coming?' Rob asked as I thrust out my hand to grab the handrail.

'Yes,' I gasped as I waited for it to pass over.

Thankfully, the staff in the blood department were brilliant and within minutes they'd managed to take enough blood.

'I can't believe I've got to climb up those bloody stairs again!' I moaned as I shuffled along like an old woman.

My labour progressed quickly but I soon realised the ward was understaffed. All I had was the student midwife which made me even more anxious.

'Are you on your own?' I gasped in between contractions, 'Isn't there anyone else up here to help you?'

The student shook her head but I could tell she was only half-listening.

'Right, I think we need to break your waters,' she decided.

As soon as I saw her approach with what looked like a crochet hook, I slid away from her and up the bed.

'Just hold still while I break your waters. It won't take a moment.'

I was absolutely petrified – petrified that she'd cut my baby open with the vicious point. But she did break my waters and, shortly afterwards, our son started to make his way into the world. As his head crowned the pain became unbearable.

'Please, I need some pain relief,' I begged.

The midwife gave me a pethidine injection straight into my bottom. The labour had been arduous and, I didn't realise it then, but my baby had gone into shock. As soon as our son Diezel appeared she realised something was wrong and pressed the alarm. Within seconds the room was full of medical staff – both doctors and midwives. Panic filled the room as I caught sight of my son's lifeless and limp body being passed from one person to another. He was a horrible shade of blue and didn't appear to be moving. I held my breath and waited for his cry only there wasn't one, only the voice of the doctor.

'Come on baby, come on baby,' he was saying from the side of the room as a nurse held an oxygen mask over my son's face.

I wanted to scream but I was too frightened. Instead I started to cry and pull at Rob's shirt as I begged him for information.

'He's dead, isn't he?' I wept.

My eyes darted from Rob to the baby and back again but the more I looked at my son, the more I was certain he wouldn't pull through.

'Come on baby, come on,' the doctor's voice repeated as other members of the team looked on.

The doctor turned him onto his side and rubbed his back whilst a midwife continued with the oxygen, but he looked so cold and blue. All I wanted to do was take him and hold him in my arms. I began to sob. They were so desperate they ached at my ribs and tore at my heart. I'd been proved right – the worst thing had finally happened.

'Hayley, look at me.' It was Rob. He was holding my face in his hands, turning it towards him to stop me from looking at our lifeless son. He was trying his best to keep me calm.

'He's going to live, Hayley, I promise,' Rob said, but I noticed he had tears in his eyes.

'He's dead, he's dead,' I wailed, my words rising to a scream.

I was sobbing uncontrollably when it happened, when our baby boy finally gasped and started to cry. It was only a tiny noise but it was enough. The collective sigh of relief in the room said it all – our baby was alive! When they finally handed Diezel to me I cried only this time they were tears of joy. I couldn't believe he'd pulled through. Afterwards, a senior member of the team came over to speak to us. He explained that Diezel had gone into shock.

'He's okay now but we'll keep an eye on him.'

I thanked the doctor for his time. As I did, I noticed the student midwife loitering at the back of the room looking awkward. I shot her a hateful stare.

*You bitch,* I thought bitterly. *You almost killed my baby!*

I remembered how it'd all gone wrong from the beginning when she'd fumbled, trying to take my bloods.

*You can't even take someone's blood, so how on earth do you think you can deliver a baby?*

Looking back, I don't think she should have been left in charge of me, yet she was. All it did was reinforce my belief that there was danger everywhere and I'd been right to worry.

Although it was a much nicer and cleaner hospital than before, in my mind, the student midwife had almost killed

Diezel and it convinced me to never go back. The thought set me on edge and, even when Diezel slept, I refused to sleep. I had to keep alert – I had to keep him safe.

*You can't sleep because someone might steal your baby!*

Later that day, I was in bed with my curtains drawn when I heard the lady in the opposite bed on the phone to her friend.

'Yes, have you heard?' she was saying. 'I never even made it. Instead I gave birth in the car!' She whooped with laughter. 'It's true! The ambulance crew arrived but I was in full labour so I ended up delivering in the footwell of the car.'

The woman was still laughing but I was horrified. The thought of the filth and germs in the car made me cringe. I was so repulsed that it took all the strength I had not to put on my slippers and go marching over there to demand she let me wash her baby! But the woman was oblivious to my horror and was still laughing on the phone.

'Yeah, that's right, it's a company car too so I've told him, "You'll have to get that valeted!"' She roared with laughter as she went onto describe the whole scene.

*All the blood and guts in the footwell of the car!* I thought as I shuddered behind the curtains.

Later, when Rob returned with sandwiches I recounted the whole sorry tale to him.

'She said her husband needs to get his car valeted but if it were mine I'd torch the bloody thing! Can you imagine how dirty that car must be now?'

My skin crawled at the thought of it. Rob thought it was funny but I didn't and afterwards, I worried about her baby.

*Christ, I hope they've washed him properly and not just wiped him down with bloody cotton wool!*

Although the hospital was much cleaner than the previous

one, I was still completely traumatised following Diezel's birth.

'Draw the curtains,' I whispered over Rob. 'I don't want any of them near him.'

My paranoia became so great that I was convinced all the staff were a danger to him.

*They've almost killed my child so what's to say something else won't happen?*

Of course, I was being ridiculous but my thoughts and irrational fears had spiralled out of control. The doctor insisted on keeping us in overnight for observation but, as soon as I could, I demanded to be discharged. I wanted Diezel back home because at least there I knew he'd be safe. I'd look after him and keep everything clean.

When Rob returned to work my cleaning obsession returned with a vengeance. I continued to wash my hands with neat bleach and I stripped and cleaned the house from top to bottom every single day. Only then did I feel it was clean enough for my babies to live in. By this time, Calum was crawling so I upped my cleaning to another level and some days I'd spend hours bleaching the same patch of floor again and again, just to be sure. My hands would tingle – not with tanning cream but with neat bleach. Nothing was left to chance. Sometimes I was so busy bleaching, I'd prop a bottle up against Diezel's mouth just so he could continue to feed while I got on with my 'important' job of cleaning. It was madness of course, but I didn't realise my obsession had taken me over to the point where I was in danger of neglecting my son in favour of bleach.

Each day, I worked my way through five bottles of bleach but I didn't care because when my house was clean I was in control. I was pouring litres of the stuff down both sinks and the toilet. I'd use it on walls and floors when I'd dilute a whole bottle with boiling hot water. I knew the bleach would kill the bacteria but I used boiled water because so would the heat. I wore rubber gloves but even with protection, the water was too hot to even dip a gloved hand into. The smell of bleach reassured me. It didn't matter that the heat and chemicals burned my skin, throat and nostrils, because now I was creating my very own sterile world where nothing could harm me or my babies. Slowly but surely my cleaning and irrational fears cut me off from friends and family until my only friend and the only thing I trusted was a neat bottle of bleach.

**CHAPTER 16**

# IMMACULATE BRIDE

'I'VE BEEN THINKING,' Rob said one day, 'why don't we book up the church and get married?'

Diezel was just three months old and we were a proper family unit: just Rob, me and our two boys. On the surface my life seemed perfect but behind the scenes, I was falling apart.

Rob booked the church in January 2007, with the wedding set for 29 September. I was still a size 16, and I felt fat and frumpy. It only gave me nine months to lose my baby weight but I was determined.

*I need to be a size 10. I don't want to be a fat bride waddling up the aisle.*

I thought about my weight constantly until, like the cleaning, it took over my life. At least when I was cleaning I'd burn off extra calories but deep down, I knew I needed something stronger if I was going to lose the weight in time for my big day.

One day, with Rob at work, I switched on the laptop and researched the quickest way to lose weight. I scoured different websites until I'd found my answer – a special slimming aid proven to speed up the metabolism – I'd just found the answer to my prayers. At £35 a bottle, the pills didn't come cheap but I didn't care because, after only a short time, they started to work until week by week, the weight was falling off. I jumped with delight every time I stepped on my bathroom scales. As an added bonus, the tablets also acted as an appetite suppressant so, instead of a large dinner, soon I was surviving on just one meal a day.

'Is that all you're having?' Rob asked as I sat down to my small plate of food.

'Well, you don't want a fat bride on your hands, do you?' I said arching my eyebrow with a grin.

Rob laughed along but I knew he didn't care what I looked like or how much I weighed because he loved me for me. The pressure I put on myself was all of my own making. I realised that, as well as the slimming tablets, I could burn off even more calories if I took caffeine-based pills because they sped up my heart rate. Soon I was taking three slimming tablets a day along with caffeine stimulants. I started swallowing more and more until I was constantly jittery and on edge. Not surprisingly, I managed to get my cleaning done in record time. Each day, I locked myself away like a squirrel, high on amphetamines, running around the house bleaching it from top to bottom. In many ways, the buzz I got was addictive. Some days I'd wake up before Rob so I could crack on with the cleaning before he left for work and I'd still be at it when he returned home 12 hours later. My body was such a toxic mixture of stimulants and slimming pills that I found it hard to sleep and survived on less than three hours a night. As soon as Rob was asleep I'd sneak downstairs and clean. It was an addictive compulsion, like a drug.

I deliberately ordered my wedding gown in a size 10 so that I could achieve my goal. The shop owner was a little wary and advised me to go up a size.

'We can take it in but we won't be able to let it out', she warned.

'No, I'll make sure it fits. I'm on a diet,' I replied confidently.

It didn't matter that the dress was a few sizes too small because, with my stash of pills, I was certain it'd fit. I reached my target weight but I couldn't stop taking the tablets because by now, I was addicted to the high I got from them. I liked the idea of having so much energy and losing weight. However, the reality was I'd turned into a frenzied zombie. One morning I woke up and my heart was pounding so fast I thought I was having a heart attack.

'What's wrong?' Rob asked sitting up in bed beside me.

'It's my heart, it's beating so fast!' I gasped.

Rob insisted I call the doctor and I did, later that morning. Before I left the house for my appointment, I typed in my symptoms and the pill names into the internet and was stunned when I read some people had suffered fatal heart attacks. I knew I needed to tell the doctor what I'd been taking in case I needed medical attention. I'd wanted to be skinny but now I realised just how foolish I'd been.

'I've been taking something,' I explained. I felt nervous sat in front of him and also a little stupid for what I'd done. 'I've been taking something to help me lose weight.'

The doctor looked up. I had his full attention. I confessed all about the slimming pills and caffeine supplements.

'And I've been taking more than I should,' I admitted. I stared hard at the floor because I felt such an idiot.

The doctor was horrified and ordered me stop taking them straight away. He explained the mixture of tablets had caused my heart to go into overdrive.

'You mustn't take them anymore, do you understand?'

He said that while the slimming tablets were considered legal, there were plans in place to get them banned.

'They contain a small amount of amphetamine, which will have caused your heart to speed up. If you were taking caffeine on top of that, then no wonder your heart was beating so fast!'

I knew I'd been reckless. I'd not only put my life at risk, I could've caused lasting damage to my heart. I'd slowly been killing myself in my pursuit to be thin. I'd done all that just to look good in a dress.

That night when Rob came in from work I repeated what the doctor had said. He was naturally horrified and cleared all the pills out of the cupboard. But, with the wedding weeks away, I was desperate to fit into my dress. I didn't want to get fat again so part of me felt loath to give up the pills, despite the associated risks. Rob realised just how addicted I'd become and tried to talk some sense into me.

'What would I say to the boys, if I lost you? What would I say? That Mum died because she wanted to be skinny?'

I started to cry. Huge tears spilled down my face and onto the floor. Rob was right. I couldn't carry on like this otherwise I'd kill myself. Something had to give and, in the end, Rob threw the pills in the bin. The thought of my boys without a mum scared me but without the tablets I felt lost so I returned to my cleaning. I wanted everything to be perfect for the wedding so I threw myself into organising it. I asked Lucy and three other friends to meet me the day before the wedding at the reception hall because I wanted fabric butterflies fluttering down in pink and brown from pieces of iridescent thread over the tables. I was only supposed to be there to sort out the butterflies but as soon as I arrived I couldn't help myself.

'No!' I exclaimed throwing my arms in the air with dismay. 'Look at the bows on the back of the chairs, they're all wrong! They're not symmetrical!'

Everyone groaned in the room and Rob looked up from what he was doing.

'Hayley, leave them, they're fine,' he said.

But I wouldn't listen.

'Look at the state of them!' I complained, straightening them all.

But it was no good; some were too long and needed cutting, so I grabbed a pair of scissors and snipped away until they looked identical. Then I started on the furniture.

'Rob, help me!' I said, beckoning him over.

'What?' he snapped, his patience wearing thin.

'This table's in the wrong place – we're going to have to move it. Look, it's too far away from that one, and as for the chairs,' I said shaking my head with dismay, 'they're all wrong too!'

My need for symmetry was so strong that I began to move one chair then another – it was never ending.

'Right, now for these butterflies,' I said finally picking up the thread.

I asked the girls to loop the thread and tie them individually to the beamed ceiling.

'Please mix them up,' I insisted. 'There can't be too many

pink ones in a line. I need them all different lengths so they look like they're fluttering around!'

We all got to work but it wasn't long before I started to pick faults.

'No, that one looks all wrong! You'll have to do it again,' I said climbing up to untie it.

Rob had seen and had enough.

'Hayley,' he said, taking the thread from my fingers. 'Leave it, please. Go home. I'll sort it, I promise.'

At first I refused because I knew no one could make it look as good as me, no one.

'Hayley,' Rob insisted. 'Go home and rest. I promise you it'll be amazing.'

I trusted Rob but I felt uncomfortable leaving everyone else to it. I hoped and prayed it would all run smoothly on the day. With time on my hands, I went home to clean and I bleached everything in sight. It had to be spotless because the photographer was coming the following morning. My house needed to be perfect because it would be used as the backdrop for the first photographs. Then there was the hairdresser, she was coming too, then there was Dad, and my father-in-law. I didn't want anyone to think I lived in a dirty house, so I cleaned and cleaned. Later that evening, my maid of honour, Lucy, came over to stay. She'd spent hours with Rob and my sisters stringing up dozens of butterflies so she was knackered. I was still cleaning when she arrived and I carried on long after she'd gone to bed. In fact, I was cleaning for so long that I didn't realise the time when Lucy crept downstairs to find me in the early hours of the morning.

'Hayley, you need to come to bed,' she said taking the scourer from my hand.

I'd been scrubbing the work surfaces in the kitchen for hours.

'What time is it?' I asked wearily. I felt a little light-headed from all the bleach fumes.

'It's two in the morning; you've been at this for hours. You need to stop and come to bed,' she said leading me upstairs. 'You've got to get some sleep.'

My legs felt like jelly as I climbed the steps and, although I'd been wearing rubber gloves, my hands felt red raw. I glanced over at the clock and that's when it hit me: I'd been cleaning for 18 hours solid without a break. I sighed because I had to be up in just four hours to get married. All I'd wanted to be was a radiant bride but constant cleaning had left me as worn and tattered as an old maid. In the end, I drifted into a fitful sleep. By the time the alarm clock sounded I was thoroughly exhausted and felt as though I'd not been to bed at all. Wearily, I dragged myself up and made my way into the shower. I meticulously washed myself from head to toe and slathered my skin with moisturiser. I got changed into some old clothes and spent ages applying and reapplying my makeup. Even though I was having my hair done, I couldn't bear the thought of smudging even the tiniest bit of foundation on my wedding gown. I needed my face and dress to be flawless. As the hairdresser got to work, more and more people arrived, including my three sisters who were also my beautiful bridesmaids.

I dressed Calum and Diezel in matching cream trousers, waistcoats, shirts and ties but as I stepped back to look at them a thought occurred to me.

*What if they spill something?*

'Here,' I said tying bibs around their necks, 'just in case.'

Calum complained he wasn't a baby any more but I told

him to be quiet because I couldn't take the risk. I couldn't relax. I was having my hair done and monitoring the boys but inside I was all churned up, waiting for the moment when something went wrong. The hairdresser pinned my hair in place just as I'd asked but as soon as she'd left I ripped it all out again because it didn't look quite right.

'I look like Amy Winehouse,' I wailed as I took a brush to it.

'It looks fine Hayley, you look lovely,' Zara said trying to stop me.

But I didn't believe her.

'I can't wear my hair like this – it looks stupid!'

Although it seemed perfect to everyone else, I thought my hair looked ridiculous. Thinking back, I realise it was because I had to have complete control. Even when I'd restyled it, it looked exactly as it had done before but it made me feel better knowing that I'd done it. I pinned on my 12-foot-long veil and then I was ready to go, almost.

'The boys!' I remembered, 'Please don't let them spill anything on their clothes!'

My makeup was paramount so I applied and reapplied it time and time again. Soon I was running over an hour late.

'What about the boys, who's got the boys?' I panicked as Dad and my sisters tried to hurry me along and out of the house. 'Make sure they keep clean. I need them clean!'

But no one was listening; they just wanted to get me to the church on time.

'You look beautiful, Hayley,' Dad said as I climbed into the back of the wedding car. He dipped his head and gave me a kiss on the cheek.

'Do I?' I asked. I was genuinely surprised because I didn't feel it – that was the problem, I never felt good enough.

It sounds strange, but as soon as we left, a feeling of calm enveloped me and I felt okay. It was as though the house held it all inside – my problems, obsessions and insecurities – they were all in there, waiting for my return. For a few hours at least, I prayed I'd relax and enjoy my special day. The wedding was amazing and, as soon as I saw Rob, I knew it was what I wanted more than anything else in the world. Although everyone was looking at me, today it didn't matter because today I was going to become Rob's wife. Against all odds, I fitted into my size 10 wedding gown. To the shop owner's amazement, she'd even had to take it in a size because I'd lost so much weight. When I finally said 'I do' I was the happiest woman on earth. It was only later at the reception that the same old insecurities slowly crept back in.

'Just nipping to the loo,' I whispered to Rob as I grabbed my bag.

I stood in front of the mirror and re-did my makeup. I applied bronzer to my face and body, a little more mascara, lipstick and finally a slick of lip-gloss. But it didn't look right so I did it again, and again. I had to look my best – I had to be an immaculate bride. The more I stared at my reflection, the more flaws I noticed. My hair was all wrong. It'd been neatly pinned back but now it looked awful. I tugged a few bits down until they hung around my face. But a short time later, I was back there again. Now my hair looked messy so I took it all down and changed the style.

'There,' I said looking at my reflection in the mirror, 'much better.'

I applied more lipstick, touched up my mascara and left the toilet. But it wasn't long before I was back again. My hair looked limp so I pulled out some pins and attempted to put it back up again. Whatever I did, I still wasn't happy. Soon, I'd spent as much time in front of the mirror as I had mingling with my guests. The worst thing was, I'd not even realised because to me this was normal. It was normal to change and reapply my makeup dozens of times. It didn't even matter that the longer I spent in the toilet, the more of my own wedding I missed because I couldn't stop and I didn't know how to.

# CHAPTER 17

# *COMING CLEAN*

WE HAD OUR honeymoon at Butlins, followed by a week in a caravan at the coast. It was hardly the Caribbean, but with two small children and with me unwilling to allow anyone else to look after them, Rob had very little choice other than to go along with it. Despite the weather, we had a lovely time but soon enough, it was back to reality.

A month after the wedding, Rob's mum invited us over for a barbecue at her house. I was already determined not to eat anything. It wasn't anything to do with Kay or her cooking but everything to do with me. True to form, before we left, I insisted on cleaning the house first.

'Does it really matter?' Rob asked, a little exasperated.

But I'd already pulled on a pair of rubber gloves and had the scourer in my hand. Still, the fact he'd questioned me was enough to set me off.

'Yes, actually Rob, it does!'

Rob had married me. He thought he knew me but he didn't, not really, because I'd hidden my behaviour from him. He knew I didn't like mess but he didn't realise I physically couldn't bear to leave behind a dirty house, not even for a few hours.

*He's a man,* I thought. *He doesn't care about stuff like this, I do.*

However, an hour or so later I was still there on my hands and knees scrubbing the kitchen floor.

'Hayley, can't this wait?' Rob asked, rolling his eyes. He was standing holding Diezel in his arms. He'd dressed both boys and they were ready to go.

'Oh, in a minute!' I said in a fluster as I tried to remember which square inch of floor I'd just scrubbed.

More time ticked by and I was still at it, this time scouring the kitchen cupboards and work surfaces.

'Hayley, we really haven't got time for this, we're already late, come on!' He was beginning to lose his temper.

'I'm almost done!' I sang, as my anxiety finally started to lift.

I glanced around – everything was clean and gleaming. I took a deep breath and let out a sigh because somehow, I'd managed to do it all. I made a mental note inside my head as I recalled each room. I'd scrubbed the kitchen and bathroom floors, the cupboards were done, along with the worktops, and I'd bleached both sinks, too. I'd even scrubbed out the bath. I mentally ticked each and every one off my checklist.

'All done!' I said, finally putting down the scourer and throwing the empty bleach bottles in the bin. I'd used two in the past hour alone.

'I just need to redo my makeup,' I called as I nipped upstairs to get my bag.

'That's it!' Rob snapped, grabbing Calum's hand, 'We'll wait for you in the car.'

My makeup didn't look too bad but I gave everything a quick touch up and added another layer, just to be sure. I had to look perfect – I hated it when he rushed me like this.

'Hayley, come on!' Rob called through the open window of the car. He'd left the front door ajar and I could hear him revving the engine on the driveway outside.

'Okay, I'm on my way!' I hollered, giving my lips one last slick of lip-gloss.

I felt content as I pulled the front door closed behind me. I'd cleaned the entire house from top to bottom and, now I'd completed my routine, I could go off and have a lovely day with my three boys. I was satisfied because now I was able to relax.

Rob watched as I'd climbed into the passenger seat and pulled down the interior mirror. I searched inside my makeup bag and felt relieved when my fingers located my mascara.

'Err, I thought you'd just done your makeup?' Rob said, still watching me.

'I have, I just want to touch it up a bit. Why, is it against the law all of a sudden?'

'No, it's just that we're already well over an hour late and Mum is going to wonder where we've got to.'

I rolled my eyes and turned back towards the mirror.

*You can be a real nag when you want to*, I thought as I applied another layer of mascara.

Rob pulled the gear stick into reverse and backed out of the driveway. Moments later we were sailing along the main road but, as I coated my lashes with mascara, a terrible thought occurred to me. My heart thumped and my palms felt clammy with sweat. I knew it'd make us even later and Kay would be annoyed but it was no good, I'd forgotten to do the most important thing! We had to go home.

'Rob,' I gasped. 'You've got to turn the car back!'

'What? Why? We can't, we're already late!'

He fixed his eyes on the road ahead with a steely determination; whatever it was, he was determined to keep going.

'Rob, please!' I begged. 'I've got to go home NOW because I've forgotten to bleach the toilet!'

Rob looked at me as if I'd completely lost my marbles. I didn't care, all I could think of was how could I have forgotten to clean the dirtiest thing in the house?

*What had I been thinking?*

I begged and begged until, after what had seemed like an eternity, Rob finally clicked on the indicator and slowed the car down at the side of the road.

'Are you serious? Do you really want me to turn the car around so you can go back and bleach the bloody toilet?' His voice was incredulous.

'I know it sounds mad but I have to do it. I have to go back!' I said, hoping he'd understand.

Rob shook his head in both annoyance and disbelief.

'Look, we're already running late because you had to bleach the bloody kitchen,' he said banging his hand against the steering wheel in a temper. 'And then you had to stop and do your makeup, again. Hayley, it's a toilet, it can wait!'

But my anxiety levels had built up inside and it came spilling out of me in huge frightened sobs, as tears streaked down my face. The boys looked at me, their little faces crumpled with concern, as they watched their mother have a breakdown in the front of the car.

'You don't understand. I've GOT to go back! I've GOT to

bleach it otherwise it'll be dirty and bacteria will grow. Rob, I'm begging you,' I said, desperately tugging at his arm. 'Please can we go back? It'll only take a minute, I promise.'

My face was a complete mess and mascara had streaked down it like angry black claw marks. I was so distraught that I'd upset the boys so Rob gave in. He knew it was one argument he wouldn't win. If he hadn't turned the car around, I'd have got out and walked the last few miles home to bleach the toilet – Rob knew it and so did I. The car signalled and turned in the road. As soon we pulled into our street and I saw the house I felt better.

'Thanks,' I said as I unclipped my seatbelt and dashed inside.

My eyes darted around the kitchen looking for my rubber gloves. Thankfully, they were exactly where I'd left them, neatly folded on the side of the kitchen sink. I bobbed down, thrust a hand inside the cupboard, and retrieved a fresh bottle of bleach. The weight of it in my palm reassured me as I ran up to the bathroom and headed for the toilet. I pushed and twisted off the safety cap and poured the thick golden liquid directly into the bowl. I watched as it drained downwards from underneath the rim, killing everything in its path. But I still took the toilet brush and gave it a good scour, for extra measure.

*Almost done.*

I poured in more bleach and repeated the same process again. The bottle felt lighter as chemical vapours filled the air. I inhaled them and the fumes burnt and caught at the back of my throat. As it stole my breath I felt satisfied that I'd done enough. It was okay to leave because the house felt safe again – there were no bacteria left because the bleach had eradicated them.

'Done?' Rob snapped as I climbed back into the car and fastened my seatbelt.

'Yes,' I smiled. 'Right, it's fine. Now we can go.'

And I felt good. I felt good because I'd left nothing to chance. I was aware of Rob watching me as I pulled the mirror down and applied more makeup. I knew he was staring but I ignored him.

*I was a young girl who wanted to look good for her husband,* I reasoned. *What was wrong with that?*

Despite my worries, I enjoyed the barbecue. It was a red hot day and there was lots of food. Luckily, I managed to put a bit of salad on my plate, which I pushed around with a fork to make it look as though I was eating. In the end, I took a piece of chicken and sat at the end, next to the wall. I pulled my hair around my face so no one saw me nibble it. By the time we returned home it was late so we put the kids straight to bed. I was exhausted too so I was glad the cleaning was done for the day. The following day was a Sunday and the boys were still in bed but as usual, I was up early to clean. Rob came looking for me; he seemed on edge as though something was bothering him.

'Hayley, can I speak to you?' he said.

I looked up a little startled. Rob sounded different. My stomach knotted. Something was wrong.

'What's the matter?' I asked. I looked at Rob but his face was stony and serious.

'I need to talk to you about something', he said, gesturing his hand over towards the sofa for me to sit down.

My heart sank. I'd never heard him sound like this before, it worried me.

'What? What is it?' I gasped.

I thought of the boys but they were both tucked up in bed so I knew it couldn't be them. Rob contemplated what he was going to say. Whatever it was, I didn't want to hear it. He rubbed his forehead and absentmindedly ran his fingers through his hair as he began to speak.

'Hayley, do you think the way you reacted yesterday was normal?'

The breath I'd been holding came rushing out.

*Is that what this is all about? Oh thank God! For a moment I thought you were going to tell me you were leaving!*

I was so relieved I could barely comprehend what he was talking about.

'What do you mean?'

I was totally flummoxed. I thought back to the day before.

*What had happened? Had I said something, had I upset someone in his family? What the hell was he talking about?*

Rob cleared his throat and began to explain.

'The toilet, Hayley. The way you made me turn the car around so you could come back and bleach it. Do you think that's normal?'

'What?' I said almost laughing, but inside I felt a little shocked and offended.

Now it was Rob who was being ridiculous!

'What? Is this what this is all about, just because I wanted to clean the bloody toilet? Yes, I do. I do think it's normal to want to clean the toilet,' I snapped defensively.

The whole conversation would have been laughable if Rob hadn't been so serious.

'Well, I'm telling you now, it's not normal. Making me turn the car back to bleach the toilet, that's not normal!' he insisted, taking my hand in his.

I looked at him as though he'd just slapped me across the face.

*Of course it was normal! That's what mums did; they kept the home clean, for their children, to stop them getting contaminated, to stop them from getting ill, to stop them from dying!*

I tried to argue my case but Rob refused to listen.

'Hayley, I love you, but I don't think you're very well. I think you've got post-natal depression or something. You need to book an appointment with the doctor tomorrow. You need to talk to him about this. I'll come with you – he'll know what to do.'

I felt humiliated.

*I wasn't ill! I was absolutely fine. This was Rob's problem, not mine!*

I snatched away my hand, utterly insulted.

*What are you trying to imply?* I looked at Rob as though I was seeing him for the very first time.

*Is that what you really think of me? I cook, clean and look after your children but now because I do all that you think I'm ill? It wasn't me who was barking, it was Rob!*

'I'll come with you. I'll help you explain,' he was saying.

But I didn't need him or want him with me because there was NOTHING to explain. Despite my protests Rob refused to back down.

'Okay,' I said finally, trying to humour him. 'I'll go, but you'll be the one who'll be embarrassed when we speak to the doctor because it's YOU, not me. It's YOUR problem because you've not been brought up properly, you're not clean enough!' I spat out the last few words as though they were venom.

'I'll book an appointment then, shall I, with the doctor?' Rob said, his voice sounding lighter than before.

Within seconds my annoyance had turned to anger.

'Anyway, I only do it a couple of times,' I reasoned.

*There was nothing wrong with me, this was all Rob – he was looking for things now.*

I turned and walked away from him so he didn't see my face. Inside I was crippled with embarrassment because I knew he'd sussed me out. But there was something else, I was frightened, frightened that between them, Rob and the doctor would make me stop and if I stopped then something bad would happen.

The following morning I felt a little foolish when we walked into the doctor's surgery. I gave my name at reception and shot Rob a hateful stare.

*I can't believe you're making me do this. I can't believe you're showing me up like this.* I cursed as I took my seat.

'It's all his fault – he's the one who made me come here,' I told the doctor as soon as we walked in the room. 'There's nothing wrong with me, it's him.'

I was hot with both anger and shame. We were wasting the GP's time on something which didn't matter, something trivial. But the doctor wasn't listening to me.

'Please take a seat,' he said, pointing over towards two chairs.

Rob sat beside me and, for the first time in my life, I felt so small that I could barely speak. I'd wanted to say so much because I knew I was on 'trial'. But I'd done nothing wrong. If anything, Rob had the problem, not me! I tried to explain why Rob had brought me there but at the same time, I downplayed everything in front of the doctor.

'I do clean, but I only do it a couple of times a day,' I insisted. Rob butted in.

'No you don't, Hayley; you do it all the time. You wash

your hands with bleach, you clean and scrub every inch of the floor.'

I flushed bright red as he relayed it to the doctor, even the part where he'd turned the car around so I could go back to bleach the toilet.

*I knew you'd mention that bit,* I thought bitterly.

I half expected the GP to stop him mid-sentence and tell the both of us to clear off and stop wasting his time. Only he didn't. Instead, he nodded and listened. Occasionally, he looked over from Rob to me and back again. The more I heard, the more ridiculous I knew I sounded. I'd been cleaning non-stop for years but I couldn't hide it any longer – my dirty secret was out in the open. I was terrified the doctor would make me stop. If I stopped then I wouldn't have control. I had to do something; I had to beat Rob at his own game so I played down everything he said.

'I only clean a few times. Stop exaggerating, Rob!' I said, trying to shut him up. 'Don't listen to him doctor, I only clean the house a few times, honestly!'

Rob shook his head furiously; he was having none of it.

'Hayley, you think I don't know, but I do. You clean the house five or six times every day. It's out of control. It's as though you can't stop yourself!'

Anger built up inside and I wanted to kill Rob right there and then. But deep down, I was angry because he'd found me out. Rob was telling the truth – I did clean the house obsessively. I thought he'd not noticed. I thought I'd been smart, that I'd covered my tracks but obviously I wasn't as clever as I thought I was. And now Rob had become my voice because I was still trying to hide it, even from the doctor. But as it turned out the GP had heard enough.

'It sounds like you might have something called Obsessive Compulsive Disorder or OCD,' he said.

I looked up at him, startled.

*There was a name for it? There was a name for all this madness I felt inside?*

I asked him to explain and, as he spoke, two words stood out from the rest: 'mental illness'. I felt sick because I knew he'd described my strange behaviour exactly. The more he told us, the more I identified with it. Still the words 'mental illness' were there at the centre of it all like a flashing red beacon.

*Is that what you're saying? I'm mental?* I thought as I listened.

'I'll need to refer you,' the GP explained as he turned back towards his computer screen. He scrolled down a list and then spoke. 'There's an outreach team, but they'll need to assess you, and then you'll need to see a psychiatrist.'

*A psychiatrist!* The voice screeched inside my head.

*I was right; he did think I was mental!*

Within minutes my fears had gone into overdrive.

*If he wants me to see a psychiatrist then he must think I'm mad. That's it, he thinks I'm mad!*

I clasped my hands together gripping them hard to stop the terrified scream from leaking out and escaping through my mouth. My hands were red and cracked from all the cleaning. The more I looked at them, the more I realised what I'd done to myself. This had progressed from emotional damage into a physical one. My skin wasn't soft and lovely anymore; I had the hands of an old woman – hard and calloused. I'd maimed myself in my desire to be 'perfect'. But the thought of stopping paralysed me with fear.

*You're going to stop me from cleaning and doing all the*

*things I need to do. If you stop me then I'll lose control of everything!*

'So it's not post-natal depression?' Rob asked as though he'd not heard the doctor correctly. He seemed as shocked as I was.

Although I was frightened, a small part of me felt relieved. At least I had a name for it – a name for all the mad things I'd done over the years. It'd all been an illness called OCD. Everything I'd thought or felt I had to do had been a compulsion – for the first time in my life I could label these crazy things under one heading. But I also fretted because *I'd* been labelled – the doctor thought I was mad.

*Mental illness*, he'd called it. *I was mad and now I'd have to see a shrink!*

The more I mulled it over, the worse I felt. Then a fear gripped me. It was so terrifying that I thought I'd throw up.

*If they think I'm mental then they'll take my kids away!*

COMING
CLEAN
LIVING WITH OCD

## CHAPTER 18

# *FAME AND OCD*

DESPITE MY WORST fears, the doctor didn't call social services or take my kids away, instead he sent me to a specialist team where I was assessed and referred to a psychiatrist. Thankfully, Rob went along with me. My biggest fear was they'd stop me performing my rituals and, in doing so, they'd take control away from me. In many ways, although I'd initially feared being labelled as having a mental illness, part of me felt relieved because, after all these years, I was getting the help I needed. The huge weight I'd been carrying on my shoulders was being passed over to someone else, someone who didn't think I was mad, and someone who wanted to help. I presumed they'd make me stop overnight. I was terrified that if I didn't complete my daily rituals then Calum or Diezel would die. But as I looked down at my hands, red raw and peeling, I realised I needed to be stopped. I lifted them up and showed them to the psychiatrist.

'This is what it's done to me,' I told her. 'This is how my OCD had damaged me. I clean my hands with neat bleach up to 60 times a day. It's painful and exhausting and this is the result.'

The psychiatrist looked from my parched fingers back towards me. I felt scared.

*Surely if I'm this mad, then I shouldn't have kids? What if they took my kids away?*

But the more I spoke about my fears and compulsions, I realised just how ill I'd been. Despite my worries, talking to professionals helped me see my life clearly for the very first time. I wasn't a bad person and my house wasn't as dirty as I imagined it to be. Although they were both fears, I realised they were locked inside my head. It was as though my brain was stuck on the same thoughts, playing them over repeatedly. But it wasn't just about me. They asked Rob how my illness had affected him and it shocked me when I realised how upset he was just talking about it.

'The truth is I can't cope with it anymore. It's getting too much, it's getting out of control because she constantly worries about the house, the kids and the way she looks. I just can't cope,' he confessed.

I hadn't known he'd felt like that but he'd suffered just as much. This wasn't about me; this was about my family and the effect my OCD had had on them. If anything, it made me even more determined to see my treatment through and get better. The more openly I talked, the more my irrational worries eased. I felt better because I knew I was going to get help and then maybe, just maybe, all these thoughts, fears and rituals would come to an end. I realised, by looking at my problems from a different perspective, how irrational I'd been. I had to accept help because my OCD and rituals had put a strain on my marriage. If I didn't get help then I'd lose the man I loved. I understood just how extreme my OCD had been. I was so bad that if Rob had left a sock lying on the bedroom floor it'd feel like the end of the world because my OCD exaggerated everything to the point where I'd scream and shout.

I remembered one day Kay coming over to the house to try and act as peacemaker because Rob and I had been having terrible rows.

'I hate everything. Everything he does annoys me... even the way he breathes,' I confessed.

Kay looked at me a little shocked.

'Well, Hayley, even he can't stop the way he breathes.'

Despite our differences, Kay was just trying her best to help but I refused to listen, just as I'd refused to listen to them all and had done, until now.

We met with a psychologist, who talked me through my rituals and asked Rob how he felt. The psychiatrist and psychologist then met to discuss my case and, by the third meeting, I was formerly diagnosed with Obsessive Compulsive Disorder. I felt an overwhelming sense of relief. It was good to have a medical name for the thing which had plagued and almost destroyed my life. I still cleaned the house from top to bottom but, with therapy, I tried to address my ritualistic behaviour. It was a slow process and one, in many ways, which is still ongoing but, after years of stress and anguish, I could finally see light at the end of the tunnel. The doctors prescribed fluoxetine, an anti-depressant, to lessen my anxiety and help heal my mind. Although it was slowly making me better, the illness convinced me the tablets were making me fat. I'd read on the internet that they were given to people suffering from anorexia nervosa. I convinced myself that they gave them the pills to help them gain weight so I spoke to a GP.

'Yes, we do prescribe fluoxetine to people suffering from anorexia but it's also given to people with OCD,' she said.

I was horrified, but the doctor explained I needed the medication to help restore the chemical imbalance inside my brain. To make things worse, I learned I was on the maximum dose. It took a good six months for the medication to kick in but it didn't feel quick enough so I upped the dosage.

*The quicker they worked, the quicker I'd get better and then I could stop taking them.*

I was supposed to take three tablets a day but often I'd double up in the hope it'd work quicker. I was delighted when I finally started to feel better. The strain on my marriage lessened too and now Rob and I lived in calm, albeit spotlessly clean, house. It didn't take away my intrusive thoughts; it just softened the blow a little. But the fear that the tablets were making me fat was still there. Mentally, I was healing but physically, I'd never felt more disgusting. Despite this, I decided to put myself out there – to push the boundaries. Getting well again became my new obsession and I wanted to see just how far I could push myself.

I'd always had a burning desire to work in TV and, despite my OCD, the dream had never gone away. But now I had even more reason to put myself in front of the world because now I wanted to highlight my illness. I was spending less time cleaning so I had more time to browse the internet looking for suitable opportunities. I scoured it looking for possible jobs and applied for ones I didn't have a chance of getting. With no experience and a mental illness, I knew I was hardly going to be first choice but, in a strange way, it spurred me on because I wanted to make a success of my life. I was a young mum with two children but I had no qualifications or experience. All I had was me – the real Hayley – the one with OCD, the newly diagnosed sufferer, who wanted nothing more than to spread the message and help others. Just as I'd been with my cleaning, I was manic in my approach and emailed every TV company I could. Surely there had to be an opportunity for someone like me? In a bid to realise my dream, I signed up with a TV agency so I'd hear of any jobs going. My chance came sooner than I thought.

One day I was at home cleaning the house when I decided to look on the website. Sure enough, a TV opportunity flashed up on screen.

*Do you want to star in the next* Big Brother *TV series?*

I nodded my head. That was exactly what I wanted. I hadn't got a media studies degree and I hardly had a GCSE to my name. In many ways, I felt as though I'd missed the boat but I wanted this – I wanted to be famous.

*I'll show them*, I thought. *I'll prove them all wrong – I'll get on TV!*

I filled out an application and, when it came to the part where I had to write a little bit about myself, I spoke honestly of my battle with OCD. I'd seen a previous series with Pete Bennett, a man who suffered with Tourette's syndrome. He'd not only taken part, but had gone on to win. At the same time, Pete had bravely flown the flag for other sufferers and helped raise awareness of what was then a very misunderstood affliction.

'If he can do it then so can I.' I re-read what I'd written and clicked the send button.

Unlike before, this time I received a phone call asking me to attend an audition. In the meantime, I spoke to my psychologist who warned me against it.

'There's no way you could live in a house with lots of other people when you suffer, as you do, from OCD. It will not help you.'

But I ignored her advice because I was determined to succeed. In many ways I'd convinced myself I was already half way there and maybe this, just this, would be enough to completely cure me.

'No one's going to stop me,' I told Rob, 'I'm determined to do this.'

And I was. Like my compulsion to clean, my desire to become famous and make my family proud had all but consumed me. But on the day of the audition I was wracked with nerves and self-doubt.

'What if they don't like me? What if I make a fool of myself?' I panicked.

*Come on, you can do this!* The voice inside my head said, spurring me on.

*I knew I'd be totally out of my comfort zone but maybe that's just what I needed? Maybe I'd spent far too long wrapping myself up, cocooned inside my house with my scourers and bleach?*

Fired up by my new-found sense of purpose, I climbed into the passenger seat and Rob drove me to the train station.

'Good luck', he said, giving me a hug and a kiss.

I felt comfortable in Rob's arms but I knew I had to do this. I knew I had to face my fears head on. I'd been reluctant to leave the house over the past few years but now here I was applying for a part on a national TV show – it was madness.

As soon as I entered the studios I stole a breath. There were hundreds of people waiting inside. Some were friendly and welcoming, eager to chat and share experiences while others were nasty, competitive and aloof. I spoke to everyone although I didn't tell them about my OCD because the producers told us to keep our personal lives just that for the time being. Also, I wanted it to have an impact: I needed people to listen because I owed it to others who were suffering with OCD in silence. Most of all, I owed it to myself.

At my first audition I had to stand on a chair and give a short speech to around 100 people. My palms were sweating and my breathing laboured. Climbing up onto that chair with so many pairs of eyes watching me felt like climbing a mountain in slippers but I knew I had to do it. I had to make myself well again. My voice stuttered as a hush descended around the room and I wracked my brains what to say.

'Err,' I said gulping back my nerves. I could do this and I would. 'I think I'll be good in the *Big Brother* house because I've got two sons so I could be the mum of the house.'

A few people chuckled, it gave me confidence.

'I'll be honest with you all, I can't cook, but I'm really good at making spaghetti!'

A peal of laughter echoed around the room.

*They liked me!*

I waited for the laughter to subside so I could hit them with the punch line.

'So... we can all eat spaghetti!'

Everyone laughed. I felt brilliant because not only did they like me, they thought I was funny too! By the time I climbed down I felt ten feet tall. I was thrilled when a member of the production team called me later to say I'd reached the next stage. For me it was vindication that I was doing the right thing. I returned to the studios only this time there were 50 people there. We were told to form a circle with our chairs as everyone took it in turns to stand in the middle and tell the rest of the group one truth and a lie about themselves. When it came to my turn, I felt my legs wobble as I walked into the centre. It was my worst nightmare with everyone looking at me I was simply terrified but, at the same time, I was determined.

*My life is going to be like this from now on, I'm going to have to push myself to the limit.*

I wasn't sure what I was even going to lie about, and then I remembered my false eyelashes and heavy makeup.

*They're all going to laugh at you because you're ugly,* the voice inside my head jeered. *They'll think you're weird and no one will want to talk to you.*

I shook the negative thought from my head, took a long deep breath and began to speak.

'Not many people know, but my cousin is Katie Price. The second thing I'd like to tell you about myself is that I've got OCD. It's a mental illness called Obsessive Compulsive Disorder, which makes me clean and carry out repeated rituals. I've only recently been diagnosed but I'm trying my best to get better.'

I watched as members of the production crew scribbled down notes on clipboards. Although my hands were trembling, the fact that people sat and listened gave me strength. This was something I could do – something I was good at. By the time I'd finished, you could almost hear a pin drop. I felt all eyes on me as I walked back in silence to my chair and sat down.

It was only when everyone had finished that members of the group turned to ask me something.

'So, which one's true then?' a boy sitting nearby said.

I scanned their faces and realised that they'd fallen for the Katie Price lie.

'The OCD, of course,' I replied, thinking it was obvious.

They were stunned because they'd already made their minds up I was Katie's cousin.

'No way!' a girl gasped. Her reaction was so unexpected that it made me look up.

'It's true.' I explained. 'I have OCD. I've had it for years but I've only just been diagnosed which is why I'm trying to do this show – I want to help spread the message.'

'But you look so...' the girl's voice trailed off but I knew what she was thinking, what they were all thinking.

'Normal?' I offered. 'I know. People don't realise what it's like unless they go through it themselves or know someone suffering with OCD because it rules and ruins lives.'

I turned back towards the girl who was still taking me in. 'Why?' I asked. 'What do you think people with OCD look like?'

I wasn't being nasty, I was just intrigued.

'I don't know really. I just didn't expect them to look like you. Anyway,' she said trying to move on, 'I think you're really brave – not only to have just done that but to have come here today.'

I was a little shocked when she got up from her chair and came over to give me a hug. The others did too. It felt amazing because I knew they accepted me for who I was, even with my illness. I admired the girl's honesty because I knew I'd come up against that sort of discrimination again. Later, I thought about what she'd said: that I looked too 'normal' to have a mental illness. I did, but now I'd made them all think about it. It'd been a good day. I felt empowered because for the first time in my life, I'd been true to myself. If I'd been worried others would judge me or write me off as a lunatic, then I was wrong. If anything, the support and love I received from strangers that day overwhelmed me and confirmed I was doing the right thing. On the train home, I felt proud. Proud I'd pushed myself but mostly, I was proud I'd made other people think about OCD and what it felt like to live with such a crippling and anti-social condition. The producers had also been impressed and invited me back to talk about it.

'It's a horrible illness,' I explained. 'It affects everything including your family and friends and those you most love in the world. I wouldn't wish it on anyone, not even my worst enemy, but only by talking about it can I finally begin to confront it. Only by talking about it can I help others in exactly the same situation and show them that they're not alone.'

At the end of my piece, a few people wandered over to tell me how brave I'd been. I felt it. I was humbled in particular by a blind guy in my group. He lived with his disability but he wasn't bitter, not at all. In fact, he was the nicest person there. In many ways, although his disability was physical, I told myself I suffered from a 'disability' too, only mine was a mental health issue and not one that people could see. At the same time, his disability and how he'd come to terms with it gave me strength. If he could go through life without bitterness or self-pity then so could I. If I could be even half the person he was, then I'd feel proud of myself. Just because I had my own crippling 'disability' it didn't mean I couldn't fulfil my ambition, and right now that was to get the message out there and to encourage other OCD sufferers to seek help, as I had. I wasn't sure how far I'd get through the process but already I felt as though I'd started to make a real difference. When I was told I'd reached the next stage, I was elated. For once, things were finally slotting into place. I was even given a code, which I had to repeat over the telephone whenever the programme makers rang. There was mounting interest from journalists eager to find out who was going into the *Big Brother* house, so the producers had to be sure whenever they called that it was me they were speaking to. It was all very cloak and dagger but it also made the whole thing more exciting. My code word was 'noodle' and I was told to meet outside a tube station in London.

'You have to look out for a girl carrying a black and white striped umbrella,' a member of the crew instructed me.

'Err, okay. Do I have to say the code word?'

'Yes.'

On the day I spotted the girl with the umbrella almost immediately. It seemed bizarre that with all the secrecy and code words they'd pick such an obvious prop to make her stand out from the crowd. The girl took a handful of us down to a different studio where we were each given a number. Once inside, we were asked to speak to a psychiatrist and another therapist who checked whether or not we were suitable and, I suppose, mentally stable enough to take part in the programme. I spoke honestly and openly to them about my OCD, but they seemed a little worried. I could tell from their line of questioning that they thought I wasn't well enough to go into the house.

'You do realise that the house gets filthy inside. How would you deal with that?' one asked.

'I'd clean. It's how I get through every day.'

They glanced at one another and back at me. I hadn't convinced them. I was fooling no one but myself.

'We'll be in touch,' they said as I left the room.

They didn't give me a direct answer that day but I knew I hadn't got through. When I was eventually told I'd been unsuccessful I beat myself up about it. They hadn't chosen me, not because of my illness but because of me. I wasn't perfect enough. True to form, I punished myself in the only way I knew how. I turned in on myself and became destructive, analysing and scrutinising every little piece.

*I'm not pretty enough.* I convinced myself, so I applied more makeup and obsessed what I'd change about my face.

I cleaned too, until my fingers were sore. My OCD made me realise that I had an obsessive personality. The fact I'd been knocked back made me want to try even harder to get on TV. Again, my obsession with scouring the internet took hold and I checked every hour of every day. Looking back, the programme makers of *Big Brother* were right to turn me away because I was ill. If I'd have gone into that house as I was back then, I would've had a nervous breakdown in front of millions of viewers. Although they knew and had correctly identified me as being at risk, I was so ill and so driven in my desire to get on TV, that I couldn't see it myself. I would've been publicly ridiculed on TV but I didn't care because my obsession was so strong I'd have sold my soul to achieve my dream. Instead I searched and searched until one day, a year later, I stumbled upon something else. I didn't realise it then but my burning ambition was more about my wish to be accepted by others than any fake wish to become a TV star. In short, I just wanted people to like me. I read that Gok Wan was looking for girls to take part in a new show he was filming called *Miss Naked Beauty*. I recoiled a bit when I read the 'naked' bit but realised it actually referred to a natural beauty, and one without makeup. My makeup had been my mask to hide behind for as long I could remember. The thought of taking it all off in front of millions of TV viewers left me rigid with fear but, in my own mind, I thought if I could do this then I could do anything.

'This show is perfect,' I explained to Rob later that evening, 'because if I can be stripped bare on national TV, then I can do anything. It'll be my biggest challenge to date.'

Rob wasn't convinced but I was so determined that I refused to back down. I *had* to do this and I would.

The first audition was held in London, where I joined a group of girls who knew nothing about me or my condition. When the time came for me to get up and tell the rest of the group a little bit about myself I watched jaws drop open as I explained all about my OCD.

'I've only been diagnosed recently but it's also one of the main reasons I want to do this,' I told them candidly.

Afterwards, a few of the girls approached me. I could tell they were still a little shocked by my revelation.

'I never would have guessed you had something like that – you seem so confident,' one said shaking her head.

'That's the whole point, you wouldn't know because it's not something you can see. It's a mental illness, but I'm not alone. Lots of people suffer from it, they're just too ashamed or embarrassed to admit it because they're frightened, but getting help was the best thing I've ever done.'

All the girls were lovely. Just like before, it restored my faith in human nature. Perhaps people weren't so bad after all? Lots of them asked me questions which I tried to answer as honestly as I could. Although I found myself telling perfect strangers about different and very personal aspects of my life, I didn't feel as though they were judging me. Instead I felt supported, admired even. It was a good feeling.

A few days later, I was told I'd been shortlisted for filming which was due to be held in Blackpool. I packed my bag convinced that this was my moment – the moment I was going to be 'cured' on national TV. But life isn't a fairytale and if anything, although I was still receiving professional help, one obsession slowly replaced another. Rob drove me up to Blackpool in his brand new Mini, which he'd just picked up. Although I'd initially been dismissive, I now loved Minis, and this one in particular was a gorgeous gun-metal colour with red leather seats. As I sat in it I felt a million dollars but as soon as we arrived I felt out of place. I couldn't believe how stunning the other girls were, both with and without their makeup. My makeup, on the other hand, stayed firmly plastered to my face and instead, I found even more flaws in myself – if anything, they magnified themselves.

One day, Myleene Klass wandered onto the set. She was so lovely and charming that I couldn't help myself; I took a deep breath and marched straight up to her.

'You're so pretty,' I said, almost struck dumb by her beauty.

Myleene turned to me and smiled the sort of megawatt smile which would light up a room. She was polite but probably slightly puzzled by me.

'You're so pretty...' I gushed. 'I wish... I wish I looked like you.'

Myleene was everything I aspired to be – beautiful, thin, successful and loved.

'Don't be silly,' she said placing a kind hand on my shoulder. 'You're beautiful too.'

It was a generous thing to say and although she was being totally genuine, I convinced myself she was taking the piss.

*She doesn't think I'm beautiful, she thinks I'm ugly because I am,* the voice mocked.

I walked away from her and cursed myself for being so stupid and ugly.

*I wish I could smash my whole face and have it reconstructed. If I had an accident, then I'd be able to rebuild it. I'd be able to make myself beautiful.*

This mantra plagued me for the rest of the day. *Who the hell did I think I was? What was I doing here? I wasn't beautiful like Myleene Klass, or any of the other girls. I was horrible. I was an ugly looking person suffering from a horrible mental illness.*

There were around 30 girls there that day but only a handful were chosen to go through to the next round – the one where they'd have to remove their makeup in front of millions of viewers. As soon as the moment arrived, the palms of my hands began to sweat because I knew I'd got in too deep. I didn't want to be chosen, in fact, I didn't even want to be there. The thought of removing my makeup in front of other people made me feel physically sick. Bile rose up and caught in the back of my throat as they read some names off a clipboard. I hoped and prayed they wouldn't say mine because I knew I'd been wrong: I wasn't strong enough to go through this because I was still too ill. Thankfully, I wasn't picked. The relief was so overwhelming that I almost ran back to Rob's car.

As we walked along Blackpool seafront we passed a gypsy

who offered us some lucky heather. I was about to refuse when she said something which stopped me dead in my tracks.

'Your boyfriend drives a fast car,' she said pointing at Rob. 'You need to be careful because he drives too fast.'

She was right. Rob drove way too fast, I was always telling him to slow down.

'And as for you,' she said, pointing towards my stomach, 'You need to be careful because you're pregnant... with a baby girl.'

I looked down.

*She was wrong; I couldn't be pregnant – we weren't even trying for a baby.*

Still, I bought the lucky heather and told Rob we needed to call at Boots to buy some pregnancy tests.

'Just to be on the safe side.'

'But she's a gypsy; she probably says that to all the young couples.'

I refused to listen. She'd been right about Rob's car and his driving.

*What if she was right about the pregnancy?*

I dared to hope.

I went into the toilets of a large department store so I could do the tests. Sure enough, all three came up positive.

'I'm pregnant!' I said running towards Rob.

He didn't believe me until I showed him the pregnancy tests. Then he ran his hand through his hair in disbelief.

'So she was right?'

I nodded. We both burst out laughing and started to jump up and down with joy.

'She said it's a girl, do you think she's right about that too?' I asked, my eyes widening with excitement.

Rob shook his head.

'I'm not sure what to believe any more!' he smirked.

Suddenly a thought occurred to him and his face fell. 'The only thing I do know is that with two kids and another on the way, I'm gonna have to sell the bloody Mini!'

But he didn't mind, not really.

Although we were thrilled about the baby, I knew I'd bitten off more than I could chew with the TV show auditions because I'd been so desperate to get well. However, in the months that followed, I questioned everything until soon I was torturing myself on a daily basis.

*They didn't choose me because I'm too ugly. They didn't choose me because I have a mental illness.*

If anything, rejection hit me hard and made me worse than ever. By now, instead of using neat bleach I was mixing it with disinfectant just to make everything as clean as I could be because now I had another baby on the way. My house was so sterile, you could've eaten your dinner off the kitchen floor. But in my head it was still filthy. Mixing two potent chemical cleaners together was dangerous but I didn't care because my OCD meant I didn't have a stop button: I had nothing to rein me in. Once again, I was out of control but I didn't have a clue how to get off the mad rollercoaster ride which had now become my life.

COMING
CLEAN
LIVING WITH OCD

**CHAPTER 19**

# *LIFE AND DEATH*

MENTALLY, I WAS caught between a rock and a hard place. I knew I needed something to help lessen my daily anxiety so I turned to natural medicine. I bought Rescue Remedy – a blend of flower essences – said to help promote inner calm and wellbeing. To me those few small drops on my tongue tasted just like white wine which was an unexpected bonus. I realised it'd started to work when I felt less stressed and more able to deal with things. Then I was sent to try cognitive behaviour therapy (CBT). By now I felt stronger because the desire inside me to get better was almost as strong as my OCD. The CBT was a slow process but it helped by rationalising things inside my head – both the intrusive thoughts and the manic cleaning.

'The next time you go to clean the toilet for 30 minutes, instead of doing 30 minutes, clean for 29,' I was told.

It was a simple formula but one that I found worked for

me. As I had done before, I lessened my cleaning by shaving a minute off a ritual each day until, soon, I was gaining a whole extra ten minutes to myself. Ten minutes soon became twenty and then, I'd taken a whole half an hour off and claimed it for myself. I was slowly winning my life back, bit by bit. I realised my OCD really was just a big bully inside my head which fed off itself. The more I carried out the rituals the more my need was to increase them; it'd all been a vicious cycle. Now I was confronting my fears by lessening the time I spent acting on my compulsions and, just because I'd cleaned the toilet for 25 minutes and not 30, nothing bad had happened. No one had died or become sick. I reached a point where I'd been washing my hands with neat bleach up to 60 times a day but now I tried to do it one less time. Even though I wore rubber gloves when I cleaned, my hands were calloused and the bleach had all but burned off the top layer of skin.

It was a very slow process but eventually I was able to control my OCD instead of the other way around. CBT focuses on your thinking patterns and behaviour. Piece by piece I was able to break my irrational thoughts down into smaller problems and ones I could deal with. In turn, with that came hope. Every time I had a black or intrusive thought, particularly about harm coming to my children, I'd ping an elastic band around my right wrist. The sensation of the elastic hitting my skin somehow snapped me back into the moment – back into reality. Instead of spiralling down with my worry, I'd try and think through it. But the CBT didn't cure my intrusive thoughts and I worried constantly.

One day I was out with Rob and the boys.

*What if someone hurts or steals my children, what would I*

*do then? What if someone steals my kids and kills them? How would I cope?*

Instead and, in a bid to cope, I pinged the elastic band to snap myself back into the moment, back into reality. The fear was still there but I told myself that's all it was – a fear. I knew I'd never be fully cured or free of OCD, but the fact that I was able to bring it under control to the point where I was no longer housebound gave me a future. In a nutshell, that simple black elastic band helped save my life and stopped me slipping into a pit of despair. I knew as long as I held my little boys' hands and kept them safe, no real harm would come to them. For the first time in my life I allowed myself to relax and enjoy motherhood, instead of always thinking the worst. CBT helped me see the world and my problems through a different pair of eyes. I was still the same old Hayley with all her fears, insecurities and hang-ups but now something had changed. It wasn't a miracle cure but bloody hard work. Initially, the thought of putting down my scourer and not using bleach filled me with dread because part of me didn't want to stop. If I stopped then I'd lose all control, but cognitive therapy meant I didn't have to stop my rituals, I just had to try and wean myself off them. It was the perfect solution. It didn't completely take my fears away but lessened them to the point where I didn't obsess as much.

I stopped mixing disinfectant with bleach because I realised just how dangerous it'd been. The fumes from the chemicals wouldn't just affect me but my unborn child and my boys. So, when a friend suggested using a steam cleaner, it made perfect sense. I knew it'd sterilise my toilet but, unlike chemicals, it used only water. I asked if I could borrow it off her and, although I insisted on still using bleach afterwards, I knew the steam had deep cleaned the surface in a way I never could.

That simple device took away my need for a fog of chemicals so I went out and bought my own. It cost £80 but I knew it'd be cheaper in the long run because, instead of using five bottles of bleach a day, I was down to just one.

I was still particular about washing my hands and I still am, especially when preparing food, but as long as the surfaces and sink had been bleached then I could cope. I still had hang-ups about eating out in public but as long as I could sit at my special table facing the wall in Pizza Express, then at least I knew I could do it and try to live a relatively normal life. Slowly but surely my OCD lifted. I was able to think rationally and see things clearly for the first time in years.

As my 20-week scan approached I wondered if the gypsy had been right. As soon as the sonographer confirmed it was a girl I grabbed Rob's hand and gave it a squeeze.

'Let's call her Sienna,' I whispered.

However, after I'd left the centre, I started to doubt what she'd told me.

*Had I just imagined it because that's what I wanted to hear, because that's what the gypsy had told me?*

I was all churned up inside. Even though Rob confirmed it I still called up the centre and demanded to speak to the sonographer.

'It's Hayley Leitch, I was in yesterday. I know you told me I was having a girl but how sure are you?'

*I needed to go out and buy baby clothes but what if she'd made a mistake and I bought all the wrong things?*

'Well, we can never be 100 per cent sure,' she began to explain but said she was pretty certain it was a girl.

'Thank you,' I replied almost weeping with joy because I'd always longed for a little girl.

But the next day, I rang again. I did the same again and again until the poor woman was sick of hearing my voice. The need for constant reassurance was so great that I'd turned my question into a new ritual until I'd called her half a dozen times asking the same thing.

'But do you reckon it's definitely a girl, Rob?' I asked for the umpteenth time.

Rob looked at me as though he'd lost the will to live.

'Oh my God, Hayley, I'm going to have a nosebleed if you keep asking me!'

I knew he was right but it wasn't me, it was my OCD. In the end, I made myself go out and buy clothes for a baby girl. Although I felt more positive, I was having trouble picking the kids up from school because I was worried what the other mums thought of me. I started to push myself because I had to do it. I was their mother, I'd chosen to bring Calum and Diezel into the world and, even though I was poorly, I had to be there for them. On the bad days, I'd sit and wait in my car outside school until the very last moment but, the more I pushed myself, the more my health improved and I felt able to face the world. In many ways, it's a process which is still on-going, but I'm getting there.

My OCD was there whenever the boys got their toys out to play but I forced myself to fight the urge to tidy up. This was my problem, not theirs. I couldn't inflict my illness on them. I calmed myself with the thought that no matter how much mess they made, I'd always be able to tidy it up at the end of the day. Slowly, I began to heal.

I suffered from the usual morning sickness but I worked my way through it because I knew it wouldn't last forever.

With two boys and a baby on the way, we needed a bigger

place so we moved to a new house in quiet cul-de-sac in Nutfield, in Surrey. I loved living in a new home because it was easier to keep clean.

Some days I'd go and visit Nanny Linda. She was delighted I was having a girl because she was used to being surrounded by me and my sisters. By Christmas, I was five months pregnant and blooming in more ways than one. On Christmas morning, we called at Mum's so that we could see everyone. Nanny Linda was there at the hub of it all dressed in her favourite red cardigan. She smiled with delight as she watched the boys open up their presents, their little faces wide with wonder. We had such a lovely day. I couldn't wait until my baby girl could be part of it all.

Back home a short time later, the phone rang. Rob answered but as soon as I saw his face, I knew something was wrong.

'Who was it?' I asked as he put down the receiver, but Rob could barely look at me. I steeled myself – it was bad news, I could tell by the look on his face.

'Hayley, I need you to sit down.'

But I didn't want to sit down. I wanted him to tell me what was wrong and who'd just called.

'That was Paul,' he said trying to find the right words. 'Hayley,' he said, taking my hands in his. 'I don't know how to tell you this but it's your Nanny Linda...'

'What?' I said, cutting him off mid-sentence. I knew it was bad news and part of me wanted to block him out. Whatever it was, I didn't want to hear it.

'It's Nanny Linda, sweetheart. She's died.'

'No!' I shouted. I shook my head and pushed Rob away. 'No, why are you saying this? Please don't do this. Why are you lying to me? Why are you saying these awful things?' I jumped to my feet but as I did my legs gave way and I fell to the floor. The words hit me like a punch to the stomach. I tried to stay calm but I heard a scream – it was coming from me.

'No, she's not, Nanny Linda isn't dead!' I screamed as Rob tried to help me up. I pushed him away and ran upstairs to the toilet where I was violently sick.

Rob tried his best to comfort me but I didn't want him or anyone else near me. I just wanted Nanny Linda. I made my way to the bedroom, opened up a drawer and pulled out a red velvet necklace box which had belonged to her. I held it up to my face and inhaled the scent of her perfume. It felt good because it was like having her there with me. I took to my bed with the jewellery box tucked up close inside my arms. Every so often, I'd breathe in Nana's perfume. I wondered how I'd get through life without her. I felt so lost.

Rob checked on me constantly but I refused to leave my bed and I lay there for five days. I still don't know if Rob went to fetch it or if Mum dropped it off, but someone brought me Nanny's favourite red cardigan – the one she'd worn at Christmas – and her purple blanket. I wrapped myself in them both as grief overwhelmed and consumed me. Nothing would ever be the same again, nothing.

One day Rob sat on the side of the bed. 'Hayley, your nan wouldn't want you to be like this.'

I looked up at him through tear-stained eyes. He was right but I didn't know how to make it stop.

'What if there's nothing else after death?' I asked. 'What if this is it?'

But Rob didn't know the answer. No one did.

My beautiful Nanny Linda had died in her sleep from a massive stroke. It brought me comfort that she'd died without knowing anything about it. I was heavily pregnant with my own child but part of me wanted to die right there and then because I couldn't imagine a future without her in it to help guide me. She'd not only been my Nan, she'd been my best friend and a second mother rolled into one. Nanny Linda had always fought my corner and now she was gone, I didn't feel able or strong enough to continue the fight alone. I'd already battled against my OCD and felt as though I'd scaled a mountain but now this. I knew I wasn't and never would be strong enough. I didn't want to eat, breathe or sleep. I just wanted to lie down and die.

Rob was so worried he phoned the doctor.

'She needs to eat,' he told him.

But I couldn't eat because every time I put food near my mouth I felt sick with grief. Instead, I tried to sleep because at least when I was asleep I'd dream that Nanny Linda was still alive. It was only when I woke up and realised it'd all been a dream that I'd have to face my loss all over again.

I was told her funeral would be delayed because of the Christmas holidays. Instead, we were allowed to go and see her in the chapel of rest but I didn't go: I wanted to remember her laughing and happy, sitting in her red cardigan handing out presents on Christmas Day.

A week after her death we received another blow: Rob's grandma had died. Now there'd be two funerals.

On the day of my Nan's funeral, they played 'Moon River'. I'd chosen it because it was her favourite song and she'd sang it to us throughout our childhood. It was a small private funeral but I knew Nanny Linda would've approved. She didn't like a lot of fuss. My sister Lauren was crying her heart out and I wanted to reach out to her but I didn't know how.

'Please don't cry. Nan wouldn't want you to cry,' I begged.

But Lauren couldn't stop and neither could anyone else. Everyone was numb with grief – her death had affected us all.

Days later, we attended the funeral of Rob's nan and had to do it all over again. It felt ironic that all the time a little life was growing inside me, others had lost theirs. I was due to give birth to Sienna in just a few months but inside my heart had been torn in two because I knew Nanny Linda would never know my beautiful little girl. But I knew she'd be there, looking down, protecting us all, as she'd always done.

After my disastrous birth with Diezel, instead of returning to the same hospital I opted for the same place I'd had Calum. I hated the thought of going back but now at least I realised most of the germs I'd 'seen' before had been imaginary. As soon as I arrived at the hospital I told the midwives about my OCD.

'I'm telling you because I don't want the baby delivered onto me. I need you to clean her up first.'

If I was worried they'd be judgemental then I was wrong, they couldn't have been more supportive. As my labour pains kicked in, a midwife asked what my husband's name was.

'Rob,' I huffed as a searing contraction shot through my body but she misheard me and thought I'd said Robbie.

'Ooh, I love that name. It's my favourite. I love Robbie!'

Although I was in agony, it made me laugh and, after that moment, I decided to call Rob Robbie instead.

'That bloody midwife has ruined my life!' he complained, rolling his eyes.

My labour progressed quickly so the midwife checked me again.

'Your baby will be here by 12.30pm, Hayley!' she said chirpily.

I glanced at the clock and immediately felt sick because it

was 11am – only an hour and a half to go! Now she'd given me an estimated time of arrival, I felt my body tense up because I knew what was coming: pain, and lots of it. As the second hand ticked by, I realised I was getting closer to agony and something inside my brain clicked.

*If I don't push then the baby won't come and I won't have to go through the pain.*

It was madness, but I knew the birth time so I knew I could stop it and be in control. Soon it was 11.30am.

*In an hour, it's going to feel like someone has stuck a knife in my stomach.*

I tried to focus.

'Hayley, you need to push,' the midwife urged, but I didn't want to.

In the end, it took a good two hours longer than she'd first said and, by the time Sienna was born, they pulled the alarm cord because I became unresponsive. I don't remember much but I was later told that I'd haemorrhaged inside. A nurse injected me with something to try and clot my blood but my body had gone into shock. The midwife asked Rob if he'd wanted to hold Sienna while they worked on me but he refused because he wanted me to hold our baby first. The midwives were amazing. They stopped the flow and I was placed on a drip. Eventually, I was wheeled back to the ward but as soon the nurse lifted me out of wheelchair, I noticed my pyjama bottoms were soaked with blood. I looked across the ward. One of the other women had her partner with her and he'd seen. I was mortified. To make matters worse, one of the nurses noticed and pointed it out.

'Excuse me darling, you might want to sort that out because you're bleeding through to your trousers.'

I wanted the ground to swallow me up whole.

'Yes,' Rob hissed at her. 'She's haemorrhaged, that's why she's bleeding!'

I felt so ashamed that I wanted to curl up and die. But when I got into bed, I bled right through to the sheets. Another young nurse who'd just started her shift noticed and wasn't happy.

'I've just changed that bedding,' she sighed, grabbing my arm. 'Come on, get up, I'll have to do it again.'

I wanted to shout at her but I didn't have the strength. Instead, as I lifted my body up, the needle fell out of my arm and blood spurted everywhere – the wall, the floor and all over me. It looked like a horror movie!

'Are you alright?' the nurse asked as my legs wobbled and I put a hand out to steady myself.

'I think I'm going to fall,' I gasped.

She helped me into a chair and changed my bed without another word but it was too late, I already felt humiliated.

We decided to call our daughter Sienna Violet because Nanny Linda's real name had been Violet.

'Why don't you use your proper name?' I'd asked her once.

As she looked at me, a mischievous smile spread across her face.

'Because I'm not that keen, runner bean,' she laughed, giving me a quick wink.

I smiled as I thought back to that moment. Nanny Linda had been such an amazing person that I wanted Sienna to have something from her, even if it was a name she didn't particularly like.

Although I'd managed to get my OCD back under control, once I returned home from hospital I relapsed again and started cleaning obsessively. It got to the point where even CBT and the elastic band failed to help. At least this time I recognised the signs and, within a fortnight, I was back at the GP's begging for fluoxetine.

'I'm ill again,' I admitted, this time without shame.

I begged him to help so he put me on the minimum dose. I knew it'd take a while for them to kick in so in the months that followed I cleaned frantically. I also became plagued with intrusive thoughts. I'd given up smoking throughout all my pregnancies but after Sienna's birth I started up again with a vengeance. I took to hiding in the shed so I could smoke in private, away from the kids so the smoke wouldn't harm them. I hid in the dark, secretly hating myself. I felt fat and miserable as the voice told me my kids would get sick and die.

*I need to clean and bleach; if I don't then bad things will happen.*

I scoured and blitzed the place. It was exhausting and I was devastated because I knew I'd reached rock bottom again. I hated myself for giving into the OCD bully but I was too terrified not to do as it said because of what might happen. I realised I wasn't in a good place.

'I'm a shit mum,' I cried to Rob. 'I'm fat and useless. The house is messy!'

He tried his best to help but he knew as well as I did that he couldn't make me better – only I could do that.

When he was out at work, I started moving furniture around again. One day, with Rob at football, I moved a heavy three-door wardrobe from one room to another.

'What the hell?' he'd said when he saw what I'd done.

'Hayley, you could have hurt yourself! Even I wouldn't move that on my own.'

When I woke up the following morning my whole body felt as though it'd been hit by a bus because I ached so much. But I didn't stop because if I didn't move things then something bad would happen to the kids. It was a weird time for me. Sienna was still a babe in arms but I knew my OCD was spiralling out of control. I hated myself for being weak and giving into it. I just wanted to stop the world because now I needed to get off.

## CHAPTER 20

# OCD AND SUICIDAL THOUGHTS

SOON WE WERE on the move again. With three kids we needed a bigger property and thankfully we managed to find a lovely cottage in Dormansland with acres of land, enough for a big trampoline and a garden full of happy kids. However, everything wasn't quite as rosy with me. My constant need for reassurance had reached fever pitch until soon I was cleaning all the time and asking Rob daily how I looked.

'You look beautiful Hayley, you always do,' he told me, time and time again, but I doubted him because I doubted myself.

*He's lying. He's just saying that to keep me happy.*

Instead, as soon as he'd left for work, I'd get down on my hands and knees, mix disinfectant and bleach in a bucket, and scrub the floor until it was spotless. The vapours were so strong it felt as though they were stripping the lining of my lungs. But the harder it became to breathe the better I was because I knew it was working – I was getting the place clean again.

I searched through my colour-coded wardrobe looking at all my clothes but I hated them because I despised myself. I was fat and unattractive carrying my post pregnancy weight but I could change everything. I'd stop taking my tablets.

One afternoon, I was due to pick Calum up from school but I couldn't bring myself to leave the house. I knew the other mums would look at me so I put on a hat. But when I glanced at my reflection I realised just how stupid I looked. The thought of going to the school made me have a panic attack and soon I was in floods of tears. But it was no good, the clock was ticking and I had to leave. I was already late so, when a friend called to ask how I was, I promptly burst into tears. She was concerned because she'd never heard me sound like that before. I'd been clever because I'd hidden my OCD from everyone, but now it'd all come flooding out.

'I don't want to go to the school,' I wept, 'I've got to wear a hat because they'll all look at me. All the other mums will watch and judge. But now I look stupid because I've got a hat on.'

'Please don't cry, Hayley,' she soothed. 'Try and hold it together.'

'But I can't, not anymore. You don't understand,' I told her. 'I feel so shit about myself.'

It was a vicious circle. I'd put the hat on to cover my face but I knew it would make them look twice as much because I never wore a hat. In the end, I was fifteen minutes late and the other mums had already left. I ran into the school and straight up to reception.

'I'm sorry, but I was stuck in traffic.'

The lie slipped off the top of my tongue because I was so used to covering up. I was used to making excuses for my lateness and strange behaviour. I didn't want her to know the truth because I was frightened, frightened I'd lose my kids.

One afternoon, I was sat at home thinking about how everything had gone wrong. I'd reached a point where I didn't even want to be alive anymore. As I looked across the room I spied the brown medicine bottle on the side. I picked up the pills and eyed the contents of the little brown bottle suspiciously.

*The fluoxetine hadn't helped at all; it'd just masked things. It'd been masking my worries when all the time they'd been the real cause of them. The pills were making me fat and now I also had my baby weight to lose. If I wanted to get on TV, and I wanted people to like me, then I'd have to stop taking them. I'd have to stop right now!*

More than two years after being prescribed my much-needed medication I convinced myself I was better. I stopped overnight with no consultation, I just did it. I didn't realise it then but it was the worst thing I could do. Almost immediately, I became even more anxious than I had been before. Slowly I shut myself off from the world and became obsessed with other mums at the school. I told myself they were judging me. I convinced myself it was because I was so ugly and worthless: that's why they all hated me. One afternoon, I left the house to pick Calum up from school. I was running late because I'd been so busy cleaning, doing my hair and makeup so that I could face the world. Even then I drove with my hair draped across my face so I could hide behind it but I was still over an hour late. I knew the teacher would be there, waiting to have a word with me so I lied and told her my car had broken down.

'Oh okay,' she said, although I was certain she hadn't believed me.

But it happened again and again. Each time I'd make up a different excuse because I was too ashamed to tell her the truth, that I had an illness.

Once home, I sat there waiting for the knock at the door, waiting for someone from social services to take my babies away from me. I could just imagine Rob's face as they took our kids and carted me off to the local nut house. What would become of me then? Instead, wracked with guilt and self-loathing, I cut myself off from everyone. I put myself under house arrest because at least if I didn't go outside then no one would realise how mad I'd become. At least no one would be able to judge or hurt me or my children. I even reached a point where I thought Sienna and the boys would be better off without me.

*Rob and the kids would be so much better with me dead.*

The more I thought about it, the more sense it made. If I were dead then I wouldn't be able to hurt anyone. If I were dead then my kids would be able to have a better life without me.

*I'd rather be dead than live a life like this. I'm so tired.*

Of course I wasn't thinking rationally because I wasn't rational. I couldn't think straight because every thought and fear had twisted out of all proportion. I was trapped, locked up in a self-imposed exile inside my house and I had no perspective on the world. I'd failed as a mother, I'd failed as a wife and now I'd even failed as a human being. I was less than worthless. I glanced across the room and spotted a sharp kitchen knife in a wooden block on the side. I imagined taking the knife from its protective wooden sheath and drawing it across the thin skin of my wrist. I pictured it slicing through and into me. Slicing through a major artery, severing it until all the blood had drained away from my body and heart. Then I'd be dead and the pain gone. I'd finally be at peace. I thought of it often, of slashing my wrists, but there was one thing stopping me.

*I can't cut myself because it'll make a mess! There'll be blood on the carpet!*

Even though I knew I'd be dead, the thought was still there. My OCD was still there, even taunting my suicidal thoughts. I remembered my tablets and googled how many I'd need to kill myself. I calculated how many I'd saved by not taking them daily. I was thrilled when I realised I had enough. I could do this, I could end this torment once and for all! I devised a plan. I'd ask Rob to take the kids out for the day and that's when I'd do it. I'd take the lot, in one hit. By the time Rob returned home, it'd be too late, I'd be dead. I imagined Rob moving on with his life, marrying again. I imagined another woman acting as a mother to my children: someone normal, someone who could give them all a better life. But then I stopped. I didn't want anyone else looking after my babies.

*What was I thinking? My children needed me! How could I think such a wicked thought?*

I shook it from my head. The reality was, I didn't want to die. I just wanted the worries and rituals to stop. I just wanted to spend one day, just one day, in total and utter peace without an intrusive thought or ritual getting in the way of my life. I wasn't well, if anything, now I'd stopped taking my tablets, I was worse than ever.

On the bad days I'd spend so long cleaning that I'd forget to eat. I was too busy to feed myself but although I fed the kids, I was still too busy cleaning to be a proper mum because of the OCD. The illness had taken me over to the point where it had become the main focus in my life. Looking back, the thought of it now horrifies me, but that's how ill I'd become. I was going to extreme measures just to carry out my rituals. It was ironic because the whole reason I did them was to prevent my children from harm but now my OCD didn't allow me any time for my children.

Sienna was only three months old but I knew I needed to get a grip. In sheer desperation, I rang the clinic and spoke to a member of staff. I told them I'd slipped back into my OCD rituals so they arranged for the psychologist to do a home visit. Things had become so bad that I'd become housebound again. My grief at the unexpected death of Nanny Linda mixed with joy following the birth of Sienna had messed me up inside and had somehow acted as a trigger for my OCD. I needed professional help; I couldn't get through this alone. As soon as the psychologist arrived I told her everything – even about the horrible intrusive thoughts. I explained how I'd thought Rob would throw Calum over the shopping centre balcony.

'But why would he do that, Hayley? What makes you think he'd harm Calum?'

I knew she was trying to rationalise the thought but nothing could because the fear was still there even though I knew it was ridiculous.

'He wouldn't. I know he wouldn't. But why do I keep thinking it?' I wept.

I felt as though I was slowly going crazy. I even told her I'd worried I'd do the same thing in a moment of madness.

'And what if I had?' I sobbed. 'What if I'd thrown my baby over the balcony and killed him?'

My body was wracked with such deep sobs that they stole my breath away.

'But you didn't and you wouldn't. Rob wouldn't either, he loves his children. Hayley, this is just a thought inside your head.'

'It's not just that,' I sobbed. 'It's all the other people, I know they're looking at me. They stare at me.'

I knew I had to get back on the medication and sort myself out because I suffered daily with extreme mood swings. Rob and I took the children out for the day but when we came home, I locked myself in the bathroom and cried my eyes out. Before I knew it my legs started to tremble: the withdrawal from the pills had caused my body to go into meltdown. My legs shook so much that I could hardly stand up. I was so frightened I begged Rob to drive me straight to hospital.

'You've got to get me there, something's wrong, something's wrong with me!' I panicked.

Eventually the tremors stopped so I didn't go, but the following day I booked myself an emergency appointment with the doctor. I told him exactly what had happened.

'Right, you need to go back on the fluoxetine.'

I refused but he was adamant.

'You can't just come off tablets like that,' he said with a click of his fingers. 'You need to be weaned off them – it needs to be a gradual thing.'

Although I didn't want to go back on the medication, the whole episode had terrified me. I realised that I didn't know best – the doctors did. This time I did as I was told and started taking my medication only this time at a low dose. As soon as the chemicals kicked in, the spasms and tremors stopped and I felt human again. He dropped the dosage until I was on the minimum amount. Every day, I felt a little stronger so I spoke to my doctor about coming off the medication all together but this time under his expert guidance. He prescribed something else which I took for a couple of months and then I replaced it with the herbal rescue remedy. Finally, I was able to breathe and function normally again.

In the years that followed I managed to sort out my life and get myself back on an even keel. Things weren't perfect but I'd reached a point where I was finally managing to get my OCD under control. However, I didn't realise it then but something was waiting in the wings ready to knock me back down again.

COMING
CLEAN
LIVING WITH OCD

## CHAPTER 21

# *WASHING THE CAT*

JUST AS I'D started to cope, another family crisis hit us. We'd always known that Rob's mum and dad hadn't had the perfect marriage. Rob, his brothers, even Kay had known his father had been involved with another woman. In time, Rob's dad fathered three other children. He decided Rob and his siblings were adult enough to deal with it so he decided not to live a lie and became a full-time father to his three young children. Rob was upset, but then he'd lived a life surrounded by arguments and falling out. Although we all felt for Kay, there was nothing anyone could do. Rob's dad had chosen his new life. It was an extremely difficult time for everyone. Although we stayed on friendly terms with his dad, his leaving made Rob question everything and soon he'd even begun to question our relationship.

*Why was I so obsessed with looking good? Was it really my OCD or was it something else? Was I trying to look good for someone else?*

Of course I wasn't. I loved Rob with all my heart but I couldn't halt the new demons rising within our marriage. Just as I'd started to take control of my OCD, so the roles of reassurance were reversed and now it was up to me to convince Rob that there wasn't a hidden agenda.

One night, I was getting ready to go on a night out with my friends. It'd been ages since I'd last been out and I felt as though I really deserved it.

'Why are you wearing that?' Rob asked suddenly as I walked into the front room wearing a short dress and high heels.

'Why?' I asked. 'Doesn't it look right? Do I look fat?'

I ran to the mirror and tried to imagine what Rob was seeing. *Maybe I looked too tarty? Maybe I just looked a complete mess?*

I studied my reflection.

But it wasn't any of those things, Rob was worried I was getting dressed up to go and find someone else.

'But I'm just going out with the girls,' I said, beginning to cry. The mascara streaked down my face until it became a big, black blotchy mess around my eyes.

Rob shrugged. It was clear he didn't approve of me going out without him. Instead I ran to the bedroom and sobbed my heart out. But it wasn't an isolated incident because it happened again and again until I finally started making excuses to my friends. It just wasn't worth it anymore.

'Sorry, I just don't feel very well,' I lied.

'Oh, I hope you feel better soon, hun.'

It made me feel worse but somehow it was easier than telling her the truth: that overnight, Rob had turned from the nicest guy into a possessive husband. I felt as if it was my fault, as if I'd let him down. I had to support him through this crisis because he'd helped me through my worst. But the more it wore on, the more it ground me down. Rob started to question every aspect of our relationship until it consumed him and I reached breaking point. By February 2012, I decided I couldn't take anymore. Rob's jealousy was not only affecting our marriage it was affecting me, my OCD, even the kids. We had such blazing rows that I knew it wasn't fair on them so, I decided to leave and get a house in East Grinstead. I never lost my love for Rob, or him for me, he'd just somehow lost his way. By now, my OCD was almost under control but losing Rob felt like having my heart ripped out. But I was determined to teach him a lesson. After months of staying in, doing what he'd wanted me to do, I started going out with friends as often as I could. In many ways, I was drinking to blot out my problems. Maybe I was still grieving for Nanny Linda, maybe I was just replacing my addiction to cleaning with something else, who knows? Whatever it was, I became a different Hayley, and a person I don't even recognise. The children were still young; Sienna was three, Diezel five, and Calum just seven years old, so it was a demanding time. Rob moved back to his mum's but arranged to see them every other weekend when he'd take them out and spoil them. Although I'd never lost my love for Rob, the split had made me change in more ways than one. I was still trying to fight my OCD compulsions but now I was on my own, I began to question everything. Slowly but surely, I gave into my rituals and let them invade my life again. I didn't realise it, but I was cleaning obsessively, and then I started spending more and more time in front of the mirror, trying to make myself perfect. Inevitably, my rituals took up all my time and I was constantly late getting the kids to school. I gave the teachers the same old excuses but I could see they were wearing thin. I didn't care. On my weekends off I'd go out and get completely hammered. The more I drank and the more my OCD took hold, the less I cared until soon I was shouting at the kids. Rob and I spoke to solicitors and decided to get a divorce. The strong thread holding my life together slowly became unravelled to the point where I was falling apart at the seams. I was so desperate, I thought about killing myself again.

*I can't live like this,* the voice inside said.

And for the first time it was right, I couldn't.

But as I reached rock bottom once more, something kicked in. I don't know if it was survival instinct but, deep down, I knew I still loved Rob and he loved me. I knew I had to sort things out, to make things better otherwise my life was and would be over.

By this time Kay had met a new partner called Steve, but just as her life was moving on, mine had come to a grinding halt. I decided I couldn't carry on like this so I arranged to see Rob. We'd split up months before, but as soon as I saw him I knew we couldn't throw away what we had. I still loved Rob but that love had become twisted and warped along the way. My OCD was partly to blame because I knew it'd put a terrible strain on my marriage. I hadn't been an easy person to live with, yet Rob had supported me through it all. But my OCD combined with Rob's new-found jealousy had twisted that love until we barely recognised one another anymore. As divorce proceedings rumbled on, the more I knew I needed to save what we had. I arranged to spend time with Rob and the kids, to spend time together as a family. Slowly but surely something shifted and I knew I was falling deeper in love with

Rob than ever before. Rob realised he couldn't carry on the way he had been. Just because his parents' marriage had broken down, it didn't mean ours would. Rob was staying with his mum but she'd moved to Purley with Steve. One weekend, Rob invited me over to stay the night.

'Won't Kay mind?' I asked.

'Of course not, besides, it'll be good for us,' he said giving me a hug, 'just like old times.'

I smiled and wrapped my arms around him because I wanted to be back with Rob more than anything else in the world. That weekend, I got the children ready and we travelled over to Purley. But as soon as I entered Kay's house someone caught my eye. It was Snoop, my nemesis. He held my gaze and then he lifted his head up and pushed past. To my horror the kids ran over to cuddle and hold him.

'Snoop!' Diezel called.

Sienna followed and was running around the house looking for the cat.

'Snoopy, Snoop...' she giggled as she gave chase.

The cat loved all the attention but all I could think about was the fleas he was carrying.

*His fleas will jump onto the kids' arms and legs and bite them. If they get bitten by his fleas then they'll get sick and die!*

I pinged the elastic band against my wrist because I knew it was another irrational thought. Yet, although it snapped against my skin, nothing could convince me. Instead I tried to edge closer. Sienna had her hands all over him. Her tiny fingers ruffled his thick black fur causing white flakes of skin to rise to the surface.

'Don't touch him, Sienna,' I said pulling her away. 'He's dirty. He'll make you dirty.'

Sienna looked up in shock, her face totally bewildered. But just as I pulled her away Diezel ran into the room and grabbed Snoop in his arms.

'Put the cat down!' I said, panic rising inside me.

My palms felt clammy as I clasped them together in a balled fist.

Rob looked up.

'It's only Snoop, Hayley. The kids love him. Leave them alone, they're just playing.'

Suddenly a thought occurred to me.

'Do they play with him like this every time they stay over?' I gasped.

The thought of bacteria, fleas and dirt from the cat on my kids' skin set my teeth on edge.

'Of course they do, they love Snoop,' Rob replied.

I was mortified. All this time he'd been putting our kids at risk of germs and fleas yet, all this time, I hadn't known or even realised.

'That's it!' I said rising to my feet. 'Rob, we've got to do something. We've got to wash the cat!'

Rob looked at me as though I'd completely lost the plot. In many ways I had, only I just hadn't realised.

'No! No way, Hayley! Snoop is a CAT. You can't wash cats because they don't like it,' he said shaking his head. He turned to walk away but I ran over and grabbed his arm.

'But you wash dogs, don't you? So why can't you wash a cat?'

It made perfect sense to me.

'Hayley, you cannot wash a cat!' Rob insisted.

But I was adamant. Snoop had spent lots of time outside, just like a dog, so who knows what he had hidden in that fur of his? Who knows what was waiting there ready to leap out and land on my kids and make them sick?

'You either wash that cat or...' my voice trailed off.

'Or what?' Rob replied.

'Or I'm taking the kids back home with me. I'm serious Rob, that cat is filthy. Look at the state of his fur. He needs a proper wash – him just cleaning himself with his tongue isn't enough!'

The thought that my babies had stroked and cuddled Snoop repulsed me. The thought of cat saliva on their fingers made my flesh crawl.

'Come on,' I said, trying to jolt Rob into action. 'I'll run the bath, if we do it quickly then he won't mind, he won't even notice!'

I waited for Rob to pick up the cat because I wasn't going to touch him. As soon as he was tucked in Rob's arms we wandered upstairs to the bathroom.

'There, that's better,' I said as I watched Rob push the plug into the hole and turn the tap on.

The bath tub began to fill with fresh, warm, sparkling water but Rob looked around him as though he'd lost something.

'What's wrong?' I asked.

'What am I going to wash him with?'

I sighed, I knew exactly what we needed to use.

'Dog shampoo!'

Rob nodded and went off to fetch the bottle. I kept an eye on Snoop, who was hiding in a corner of the room. I knew he didn't like me, but the feeling was mutual. Moments later, the door opened. It was Rob; he had the bottle in his hand.

'Right,' I instructed, 'dip him in, get his fur wet then you can put a bit of shampoo on him.'

I watched from a distance because I didn't want to be the one who washed the cat: I just *needed* him to be clean.

'Meeooow!' Snoop screeched as Rob tried to dip his lower legs into the water.

With seconds he panicked and scrambled up in Rob's arms, trying to escape.

'Just dunk him in!' I called.

'What do you think I'm trying to do?' Rob snapped. 'I told you, you can't wash cats!'

'Rob, just do it!' I hollered.

Reluctantly, Rob did as I said but, as soon as Snoop felt the water on his paws, he was all legs and claws scrambling to get out. Rob looked over at me in horror.

'Hayley, I can't do this – it's cruel!'

I refused to listen.

'Just put a bit of shampoo on him, quick!' I said, sensing this was going to be a very short bath.

But Snoop was having none of it and he scratched and scraped at Rob's arms. In the end, Rob saw sense and lifted poor Snoop up. As soon as he did, he fled over towards the door.

'Grab him!' I shouted as I buried myself against the wall.

But Rob refused.

'No, Hayley. It isn't right, you're not meant to wash cats. This is your OCD.'

Of course, I was furious that Snoop had escaped a wash yet, the more I thought about it, the more I realised Rob was right. Sure, Snoop was a little dirty but probably no more so than the usual household moggy. This was my OCD. It'd got out of control again and this time I'd let it. But never again, I told myself.

*This is the last time I'll ever let my illness take over my life.*

And it was. It'd just taken poor Snoop to make me realise it. Rob had refused to pander to my OCD. He realised it wasn't helping but making me worse. The tough stance worked and, after ten long months apart, Rob moved back in. We vowed to make our marriage work not just for us, but for the kids. To be honest, the separation made me realise just how much I loved and missed him. We were like two halves – incomplete without one another. While this was a fresh start for my marriage, it was also a fresh start in the fight against my OCD. I knew I'd never be fully cured but I was determined and certain that, with Rob's help, it was one battle I would and could win.

COMING CLEAN
LIVING WITH OCD

**CHAPTER 22**

# *HOPE, HEALTH AND HAPPINESS*

Two years on and I'm still living with my OCD but now I think finally I've now learned how to manage it. I've come to the conclusion that I'll never be cured but that's okay because I control the OCD rather than let it control me. Now I can identify the triggers which make me obsess and ritualise. I know that my OCD feeds off stress and, once it takes hold, it takes me down with it. It's a constant struggle but I refuse to let OCD rule my life. The only way I can rationalise my illness is to see it for what it really is – a bully in my life – and the only way I can overcome it is to fight back. Now, instead of doing everything it tells me to do, I refuse and rationalise my intrusive thoughts.

I still keep my house clean but not to the extent I did before because I realise that was part of my OCD. If I give in and feed it, then I'm half way to letting it take over my life again. Despite popular belief, I actually HATE cleaning! It exhausts me and takes up time I could be spending with my children, but there's another part of me which wants things to be clean. That's not my OCD, it's just part of who I am. It's difficult but I've learned to separate the two. I keep the house clean so it doesn't stress me out because when I get stressed my OCD kicks back in, so it's a fine balance.

I'm still the queen of bleach and I still steam clean and then use it in my toilet but I don't do it dozens of times. It's hard not to give into the compulsion but, when I've bleached it, I simply walk away.

The intrusive thoughts are still there and they mostly revolve around my children. I constantly worry that they'll catch something or get ill, particularly from food. Whenever I cook meat I almost charcoal it, just to be sure. As for barbeque food, forget it! But I realise as they grow, there will be times when I can't control what my kids eat. I wouldn't want to because the last thing I want is for my OCD to affect their lives. It's hard but I allow them to run around barefoot in the garden and get messy because kids need to be kids. I want them to enjoy their childhood without me dictating what they can and can't do. In short, I don't want my OCD to give them a miserable childhood. I'm not perfect, but what I'd like more than anything else in the world is for my children to be proud of me. It's one of the reasons I've written this book. I hope it'll encourage and show them they can achieve anything they set their minds to; they just need to believe in themselves and their abilities. A year ago last Easter, I let them make chocolate crispy cakes. It may not sound much, but for me it was a huge hurdle. Normally, I'd insist on mixing it and spooning it into the bun cases so that it didn't make a mess, but not this time. Instead I let them get really messy! As soon as I saw the joy on their faces, I knew it'd been worth it. I was so proud that I took a photograph and sent it to Rob. It took me ages to clear away afterwards, but I didn't care because the fun they had that day was priceless!

The nature of my OCD means I still over-analyse everything. I stand outside the school gate because I'm worried what the other mums think of me. I don't interact with many, but there are a few of them I've started talking to. It's only small steps but I'm getting there. Before, I'd stand alone in the playground, continually taking my phone out to keep my hands busy, but not anymore. Now I park outside the school. On a bad day, I'll wave the boys over but I know that simple act of standing by the school gate is one step towards getting better. Soon Sienna will start in reception class and I'll have to face my fears all over again. It's my next big hurdle. The teachers won't just pass little children over so I know I'll have to go in and collect her. Rob thinks I should tell them about my illness so that they understand but I don't know where to begin. Another reason I've written this book is to try and explain to others what it's like to live with OCD. Only by talking about my illness can I ever hope to challenge and change it. I refuse to give into my OCD because I know if I do, it'll trigger the same pattern of behaviour. Once it has me in its grasp, I'll have to break free all over again. I try my best to break the cycle so it doesn't control me, but there's no quick fix and it's a constant battle, but it's one I'm winning.

Only by talking honestly about my illness can I accept it. Before, when my OCD was at its worst, I felt like a burden. I wanted to kill myself, just to be free of it. When it told me if I didn't use bleach five times on the sink, one of my children was going to die, I believed it. I believed it because the fear I felt then was as real as watching someone hold a gun to my child's head.

Like teenagers who are constantly bullied, many people with OCD commit suicide. For many, it's the only way they ever think they'll be free of it, but there is another way – and that is to ask for help. When I was at my worst, I turned to the internet and discovered an amazing charity called OCD Action. Its website helped me enormously because when other people wrote about their personal experiences of OCD it helped me articulate mine. Often when words have failed me, I used their accounts to try and explain the turmoil I felt inside. I've even sent Rob links from it so he can understand what's going on inside my head. As I became stronger and started to speak out about my own OCD, the charity asked me to write down my own story to help other young sufferers. Initially, I was worried what people would think of me but I was overwhelmed by the positive response I received from others. If, by telling my story openly and honestly, I can encourage just one person to seek professional help, then I know it will have all been worthwhile.

I'm very lucky in that I have the most amazing husband and family who have supported me through my illness. In many ways, without Rob and my kids, I doubt I'd still be here now. But I am and I want other people to know that there is hope. You don't have to live like this but it takes courage. The hardest thing in the world is telling someone what's going on inside your head. You'll worry that they'll think you're mad, that they'll judge you, but they won't. OCD is a mental illness and just like any other illness it needs to be treated correctly and often with medication. Everyone's OCD is different but I tackled my demons by facing them head on. The more I challenged them, the better I felt. So, I'd like to say this to other sufferers out there: please don't suffer in silence. It took me 22 years to admit something was wrong but it was the best decision I've ever made because now I can look forward to the rest of my life.

# *OCD ACTION*

If you or someone you know has been affected by OCD then you can contact OCD Action. OCD Action is the largest national charity helping those affected by OCD. The charity campaigns for a society where OCD is better understood and diagnosed quickly and strives to secure a better deal for people living with it. You can help by donating or raising funds for the charity, or just by raising general awareness of this debilitating condition.

Please call the OCD Action support line on: 0845 390 6232 or 020 7253 2664

You can contact them through the website: www.ocdaction.org.uk

Or write to them at:
OCD Action
Suite 506–507 Davina House,
137–149 Goswell Road

# *ACKNOWLEDGEMEMTS*

London, EC1V 7ET

There are so many people I'd like to thank but those who have helped me over the years know who they are so I'll keep it simple. Firstly, my heartfelt gratitude goes to my husband Rob for all his love and support. If it hadn't been for Rob then I would never have found the strength to admit my OCD, or to seek help. Thanks to Rob, I did. He is one in a million; somehow he's managed to support me even when I was at my very worst. I love him with all my heart because in many ways, he's saved my life. I'd also like to thank my beautiful children, Calum, Diezel and Sienna for giving me a reason to carry on in the fight against my OCD. I do it not only for myself but also for them, so that they may enjoy a happier life.

I'd also like to say a big thank you to my family, particularly my lovely mum and dad and stepdad Paul. Also, to my sisters Lauren, Zara and Jasmine and all my other family members – thank you for loving me for who I am.

To Veronica Clark, my ghost writer, who not only helped me write this book but led me through an emotional but worthwhile experience. We've shared so many laughs along the way that I just know we'll stay friends.

Finally, I'd like to thank all the remarkable people I've met during my journey, especially the doctors, specialists and other OCD sufferers. They've helped me realise that you don't have to suffer in silence; you can seek help without judgement or fear because there are people out there who can help you get better. But in order to do this, first you must learn to love and accept who you are.